SEAN DEVEREUX
A Life Given for Africa
1964 – 1993

Michael Delmer SDB

DON BOSCO

Acknowledgments

The author would like to express his sincere thanks to all Sean's friends and colleagues for their invaluable help in writing this book.

ISBN 0-9544539-9-9

Don Bosco Publications
Thornleigh House
Bolton BL1 6PQ
Tel 01204 308 811
Fax 01204 306868
www.don-bosco-publications.co.uk

CONTENTS

Chapter 1

Breaking News

And shall it be said that my eve was in truth my dawn?

The Prophet

It was Saturday, January 2nd, 1993. There was a knock on the door of my room in our Salesian House in Farnborough, Hampshire. The only other resident in the house, Fr Eddie O'Shea, was standing at my door.

Did you hear the news?
No, what news?
Sean Devereux is dead. He's been shot.
Who told you?
I heard it on the radio.

I cannot remember my reaction on that evening. The shock was too great. How could Sean, that young, vital, energetic, healthy, fun-loving, enthusiastic and mischievous personality be dead? It just did not seem possible. It just did not seem right. He was so young! He had so much more to do! He could have accomplished so much more!

I was to hear my own thoughts repeated by so many people in the following days. It was long afterwards that I read in a letter sent to Sean's parents, by someone who had known him well and worked with him and, like me, had just heard of his death on the radio,

I could not believe my ears. The great organiser and lover of children, dead. I am hurt and angry. Hurt because a good and brave man is dead, a man of substance. Angry, because the man who did the killing did not know the value of Sean.

A shared confusion.

Fr O'Shea and I spoke for some time that evening, and then I returned to my room. I think it was around 9 pm. I remember that I sat down and looked at the television. I cannot say that I was watching it. I have no recollection of what was on. Later, perhaps an hour later, the phone rang. It was a reporter from the Sunday Times looking for a quote from me as headteacher of Sean's school, and someone who had known him throughout his time there. The paper had been given my name by one of the parents who was involved in news reporting. About an hour later I received another phone call. It was from GMTV, the breakfast television programme. They said they were coming to interview me about Sean. I hesitated. I was less than confident about being interviewed. They said that they wanted some pictures of Sean, as a schoolboy, in order to give some background to their report. I must admit that I tried to put them off. I thought that they were ringing from the studio in London, but they had left London,

> Where are you now?
> We're ringing from a call box in Camberley.

They were just a few miles away, and were obviously not going to be put off! They asked me for instructions on how to get to the school.

I went to Fr O'Shea. It was now past 11pm. I needed his moral support. We went to meet the TV crew, which arrived in double quick time. We discussed where the best place for the interview would be. We tried out the Sixth Form Common Room, with a photograph of Sean, as school captain, in the background. The team was not entirely happy. Was there some more appropriate place? As luck would have it, we had one section in the school; the foyer outside the science laboratories, designated *The Liberia Corner*. One of our priests, Fr Brian Jerstice, a colleague of Sean's in Liberia, had organised a special display. It contained maps and artefacts from Liberia. On one wall was a huge display-board for photographs. Fortunately, there were a large number of photographs of Sean. He could be seen in his many activities and guises in the Salesian School of St Francis in Tappita, many miles north of the capital, Monrovia, out in the bush. They thought this background would be ideal for the interview. It was now past midnight. After the interview the TV crew thanked us and packed up to leave. The person in charge, Miss Moreno, asked me to do an interview for the early morning show in London. I was no more confident than I had been earlier. After much persuasion, I eventually agreed.

As it was so late, I had little time to get ready for the journey to London. Soon I was in the car with the interviewer, and we were talking about Sean, when she suddenly said something that has stayed with me ever since,

> You know, from listening to you and Fr O'Shea talking about him,
> I feel as if I had known Sean all my life.

Others, at different times, were to repeat this remark. This was the effect Sean had on you. My enthusiasm in speaking about his energy seemed to transmit itself to the person I was talking to. Later there was at least one other reporter, from Meridian TV, who was also enthused by Sean's energy. She expressed the wish to go to Africa to do something to help the children. I often wonder if her wish was fulfilled.

We arrived in London about 1.30 in the morning, and I was given a room in the Marlborough Hotel. I was to be picked up for the journey to the studio at around 7am. I had little sleep that night. On arrival at the studio, I was shown into a very small room in which there were other anxious interviewees. Everything here was very quiet; it was like being in a doctor's waiting room. No one spoke. We were all too nervous and too engrossed in our own thoughts, as we waited and mentally prepared for the interview.

Eventually I was whisked into the make-up room. This was quite an experience, but the make-up artists were all extremely kind and made me feel very relaxed, as they chatted. Then came the cue for my interview. Another surprise awaited me when I went into the interview room. From seeing the news on television, one imagines that it all takes place in a very smart room; far from it. There was just the background, and the sofa where the presenter sat on one side of the room. The rest of the room was covered in cameras, electric wires and other equipment, with cameramen and other assistants moving about. It is quite a shock if you are not ready for it, and I wasn't. The interview was a very testing experience, not because of the presenter, who was quite charming, but because of the enormity of this new experience. My mouth felt as if it were stuffed with cotton wool. As you may guess, speaking through a mouthful of cotton wool is not easy, but somehow I managed to get through it.

One of the questions did throw me. The interviewer said something along the lines,

> It has been said that Mr Devereux was rather reckless, and might have brought this situation upon himself.

I was taken aback and answered to the effect that I believed Sean Devereux was a person of very high integrity, who was determined, but not foolhardy. Although he was well aware of the risk he was taking, it simply was not in his nature to ignore the injustices he was seeing and experiencing. He was moved from Liberia because of his continuing opposition to the brutality and corruption of the regime, and his condemnation of the use of arms, and their easy availability

I was to hear this criticism of Sean on many subsequent occasions. It was said that he was careless about his safety and was not very diplomatic in his statements. Is there a diplomatic way to expose mass murder and corruption and the cynical exploitation of the poor? Or is truthfulness the only answer? I have always felt this way about Sean. I was even more convinced when I heard his father, Dermot, say in an interview, that if someone really is concerned about the truth, and had been brought up to always defend the truth, then how could he remain silent while all this injustice was going on around him? Surely he would have to stand up for the truth.

I left the interview room, and was taken to where the mixing and splicing is done, and given a copy of my interview. As I left I was confronted by some reporters from LWT, the weekend TV show, who asked for an interview. This I gave, standing in front of a huge window, with a view of London at dawn in the background. I was anxious to get back home. It was now Sunday morning and I wanted to go to church, and then get in touch with the Devereux family. A taxi was waiting to take me back to Farnborough.

As I entered the main gates of the school there was yet another TV crew from SW Television, waiting to interview me. I went into our Community House and did an extended interview with Tony Kerner as the interviewer. Someone came from Reuters looking for photographs of Sean, and I gave him a collection, which later appeared in various papers. Amongst these was the one of Sean on the rope bridge.[1] It became the most popular picture of Sean. His eyes are bright and mischievous and there's a roguish smile on his face. It was taken by his close friend Michael Emery. Sean and another friend are on a rope bridge. Sean is shaking the bridge, daring the friend to cross. Always the joker. It could be seen as typifying the life of Sean, ever willing to take a risk, always cheerfully challenging others to join him in a risky situation, for the benefit of young people.

Later that day I went to Yateley, to be with the family. It had been a long day for everyone who knew Sean. It is sometimes said that we remember everything that takes place on such life-changing days. In my case, that could not be further from the truth. There is so much I would like to remember with greater clarity, but I cannot.

---

[1] The picture on the front cover of this book.

I was later to learn that Sean had been shot in the back, and in the head. The bullet wound in the head was later shown to me by his father, in the funeral parlour. Dermot encouraged me to place my hand on the wound, which was covered with gauze. Although it was a horrific wound, strangely I felt great comfort in doing so.

Ironically, Sean's death took place on the eve of a visit to Mogadishu, capital of Somalia, by the UN Secretary General, Boutros-Boutros Ghali, for a peace conference. Sean had only been in the country for four months. Later, as the days went by, there were conflicting rumours and reports as to how and why Sean had been murdered. Some said he had fallen out with his guards; others claimed he had refused to pay the drivers the exorbitant wages they were asking. These were the two most common reasons given at that time. It transpired later that Sean was shot by a hired gunman. Sean was a victim of his compassion and kindness, his love of children, his convictions and his faith.

Chapter 2

Beginnings

Your children are not your children.
They are the sons and daughters of Life's longing for itself.

The Prophet

Sean was born on the 25th November 1964, in Camberley, Surrey, of Irish parents. His father, Dermot, was from Wexford on the southeast coast of Ireland. His mother, Maureen, hailed from Cork. His father worked for British Airways, as a cabin steward. His mother worked as a nurse. Sean was baptised in the Holy Ghost Church in the parish of Crowthorne, in Berkshire. He was the middle child of three children, Theresa is his elder and Tania his younger sister. Since Dermot worked for British Airways, the family was able to take advantage of the opportunities to travel, which they did, especially to Africa.

His parents tell us, that as a youngster, he was like any other boy growing up. He left his room untidy and would drive them to distraction with his games and pranks. While all the members of his family are unanimous in telling us this, they are equally adamant in telling us that you could not stay annoyed with Sean for very long. His magnetic personality drew you into forgiving him. That also seems to be the general consensus of all who knew him. However, although he had this comic side to him, he was always serious about the things that really mattered. He may have seemed gullible and naïve at times, but in the important things like integrity, honesty and truth, this was not the case.

The TV Everyman film *Mr Sean*, screened in 1994, shows a homemade movie of the family with some African children, and Sean insisting on being photographed with them. His mother says that it was clear, even at the age of five, that Sean had a close affinity with them. She recalls that once, when she came to pack their luggage for the flight home, she found that many of Sean's clothes were missing. She asked him where they were and he told her that he had given them to the children he had made friends with in the village. This early demonstration of generosity of spirit, born and nurtured in the home, was something that was to develop and mature on his journey through school and university. Maureen had always sensed that Sean had set his heart on going back to Africa.

His school friend, Paul Cowdery, sensed something similar,

> There was always something ticking over in his mind, something personal, some plan he was developing. Once Sean had decided what he was going to do, he would put his plan into action.

Sean himself was to confirm these ideas much later in an interview for his school's magazine. Asked why he went to Liberia, he replied,

Even when I was young, I had this idea of wanting to help in a developing country in some way. I knew that I could do that through the Salesian network. Since Liberia is the mission province of Great Britain, I decided to go out there for two years. But then the war broke out, and I did not complete those two years.

There is also a wonderfully evocative picture at the beginning of the film *Mr Sean*. It shows, again in a home-movie, the family in a farm setting in Ireland, with Sean carrying a young lamb in his arms. I vividly remember the first time I saw this image, I immediately thought of the Gospel story of the Good Shepherd, carrying the wounded sheep back to the fold. How typical of Sean this image turned out to be. He became the good shepherd of those in his care; he looked after them, he cared for them. In very many cases he brought those scarred by war and poverty back to the safety of the flock. He cared for those with broken limbs, broken dreams, broken spirits, and broken confidence.

This compassion for others, and the urge he felt to help anyone in need had its seedbed in his home. The very nature of his mother's profession, nursing, is rooted in compassion. His father was well known for his enthusiasm for deserving causes. When he was a cabin crew manager, he supported the building of an orphanage in Bangladesh. It required drive, energy, negotiating skills and compassion. Dermot had all these qualities in abundance and he passed them on to his son. An account of this project was given in the TV programme, *A Wedding, a Crisis and Six Hundred Children*. So it ought to be no surprise that Sean followed in his parents' footsteps on the road of service and compassion.

From an early age Sean may have had the desire of going to Africa to help needy children, but he knew that if he was to fulfil his dream he would have to get himself educated and qualified. He began this journey when he started junior school at Our Lady of the Angels, at Crowthorne in Berkshire. In 1975 he moved to secondary education at Salesian College, Farnborough in Hampshire. He was there from his 11th to his 18th year.

He was good, even very good, at many sports, representing both the school and the county, but not brilliant in any. He was a hardworking and diligent student, rather than an academic high-flyer. He had to work hard for his achievements and was quite prepared to do so. He was determined and persistent in both studies and sport, and indeed anything he put his mind to. This has been confirmed by colleagues, both at school and university. It was this determination to succeed that would enable him to make steady improvement, and formed the basis of all he was to do later in life.

He had a very pleasant manner, respecting and respected by everyone. He was equally popular with staff and schoolmates. A classmate, Richard Wilkin, recalls,

> Sean had an uncanny ability to be popular with everyone. He belonged to no particular group, yet was welcomed equally by all. It is remarkable now, reflecting back, to think that Sean never adopted mannerisms or affectation of language or behaviour that would buy popularity and acceptance. He was just himself all the time and people just loved him for it, teachers and peers alike.

Another school colleague, Christopher Lloyd, reflects,

> He was not a close friend of mine, but he did leave an impression on me that has lasted. Sean was probably the most gentle and caring person I have ever met. In the five years I was in school with him I never heard him say or do anything to anyone that could be called unkind. He was always ready to defend the underdog and was forthright in speaking up for what he thought was right. He seemed to eagerly embrace whatever was put before him, be it schoolwork, sports or whatever.

His close friend, Paul Cowdery, writing later in the School Magazine, had this to say,

> It is almost 20 years since we left Salesian College. It is over eight years since Sean's tragic death. Even with the passing years, the memories of a friend and of shared experiences remain vivid. My memories of Sean are essentially of a good friend with whom you could share a laugh, someone who enjoyed sport and someone who was immensely popular amongst his contemporaries. I first met Sean when I started at Salesian College in 1975. Although I was in a different form, Sean was one of the Yateley mob, who travelled on the school bus from St Swithun's Church. There were about 15 of us in the same year. As a group we got to know each other well. However, from the outset, you knew that Sean, without in any way being aloof, was not going to be just one of the crowd.

I hope that was true of many of us, but with Sean you never had any doubt. Although Sean enjoyed great success at school, I would not have said that his experiences were very different from those of any other pupil at any time. The atmosphere we enjoyed is probably very much the same now, an encouraging and open environment for most pupils, particularly for those of us who loved our sport! The key element was that Sean would make the most of his time.

Another contemporary, Giorgio Santoro, writes,

My key memories are simple. His outstanding qualities were his clarity of conviction and his warmth. During our years at Farnborough, I remember that Sean had an uncompromising, and deceptively simple view of right and wrong. So simple that we would often tease him, and accuse him of being naïve. However, whenever teased, I remember him always responding with warmth, and a sense of humour. As I have come to reflect on Sean's life, following our time together, I have come to realise how wrong we were in assessing his conviction as naivety. I now see that his uncompromising clarity of purpose and conviction was his key strength, and enabled him to stand up to injustice, tragically at the cost of his life.

It is remarkable that all those school friends of Sean point out exactly the same qualities: his leadership, his help for the under-dog, his compassion, his generosity, and his love of the truth.

From his earliest years at Salesian College, Sean had an open, uncomplicated and approachable manner. One of his teachers, Fr O'Shea, recalled an incident when he first started teaching at Farnborough. Fr O'Shea was in the classroom about to begin a lesson. A small boy came in. Fr O'Shea asked him what he wanted and he replied that he had just come in to *welcome him to the school and hope that he would enjoy it here.* Most youngsters would be too intimidated to do this, for fear that the teacher would suspect that they were not sincere, or they would be too scared of what the other students would think of them. That was never the case with Sean. He just seemed to accept that what he did was quite natural, and the remarkable thing is that he made it so. From his family background one can see why. In his home, hospitality and friendship were genuine, not a veneer added on to impress others. It was natural for him to feel at home wherever he was, and he acted accordingly. I think that this openly honest attitude was the quality that most endeared him to everyone.

Very early in his schooling, it became clear that he had an easy and natural gift of leadership. As he progressed through the school this gift matured. It seemed a natural progression that he should be unanimously elected School Captain in his final year. He led the school very ably and was popular with pupils and staff in equal measure. He was particularly popular with the junior students because he always had time for them. He was their hero. They would often hi-jack him and his fellow sixth-formers, and ask them to come and arrange or join in a game with them. He and his companions were always ready to oblige.

It is well attested by his peers at school that Sean was determined and tenacious in all he did, and he was very competitive. Sean always took part to win. Richard Wilkin noted this characteristic,

> Sean's intensive competitive streak was always evident. He never did things just for fun, there always had to be an edge. If he could see that you were struggling, as I always did, Sean would always help. Many summers were spent over at Wellington College in Crowthorne, or on the Yateley municipal courts, playing and chatting. Sean loved to pull people's legs, and was not above tricking me into thinking I was winning, only to play a winner from behind his back without even trying. Large groups of us would take part in matches, a testament to how Sean could bring together people who might not otherwise have mixed.

Sean remained fascinated with Africa. In 1982, while he was still in the Sixth Form he was thinking of going out as a volunteer to Africa, when he finished his final school examinations. He spoke about this to Fr Bernard Grogan, the Rector of the Salesian community in Farnborough. He in turn asked Fr Joe Brown, who was Head of the Arthur Barclay Technical Institute in Monrovia, Liberia, to speak to Sean about the possibility of his going to Liberia as a helper. Fr Brown advised Sean against this, saying that he would be of far greater help if he were to gain his qualifications in England first, as there were already plenty of unqualified helpers available in Liberia. Fr Brown told him that if he was still of the same mind after qualification, they could talk again.

Sean left school in the summer of 1982. He went to Birmingham University, in the following autumn, to read Geography and Physical Education. According to staff and colleagues, he seemed to have settled in very quickly. Sean's regime was always the same; study hard, play hard, have fun, and keep everything in perspective. In his first year at university he found accommodation outside the campus, but in the final two years he stayed at the Catholic Chaplaincy. He was Chair of the Catholic Society. His chaplain, Fr John Reid OSA, remembers him well,

> The person he was, and is, with all that energy, idealism, vision and humanity, he was already this when he arrived at Birmingham University.

Madeleine Winnett, a close friend, who was resident in the Chaplaincy at the same time, recalls,

> Obviously, from the video *Mr Sean* you can see how much Sean affected people and touched their lives, but from his silly walks, face pulling and sticking fingers up at the camera, etc., you can also see the side which Ian and I knew so well. Headlines in the papers calling him *A Saint in Shirt Sleeves* weren't synonymous with the memories I had whenever his name was mentioned. Instead, I instantly thought of Sean the comedian, Sean the practical joker.

From Madeleine's account he was a practical joker. He would bombard others with water bombs, and then try to escape the wrath of his victims. On one occasion, however, he was chased along one of the corridors by a hapless victim. Disaster threatened when Sean spotted one of the Chaplaincy Sisters, at the other end of the corridor. This forced him to make a snap decision and seek refuge in Madeleine's room. It was around midnight, and Madeleine was already in bed when he arrived. She was taken aback by the intrusion, until he explained his dilemma. When, eventually, he put his nose outside the door to see if the coast was clear, he exclaimed, *Do you smell burning?* Before all this had happened he had put some bread in the grill and now the Common Room was filled with the smell of burnt toast. Sometimes his companions got their own back. His friends once secreted a loudspeaker under his bed, and having waited for him to drift off to sleep, began to call in sepulchral tones, *S...e...a...n! S...e...a...n!* His yell was heard both above and below.

Sean was also an accomplished mimic. Fr Nicholas Latham, the Chaplain at Birmingham University, said he did a really good imitation of him, with tone and mannerisms in true caricature, but which never felt threatening or lacking in respect. Sean's companions also remarked on this gift, another string to his bow in keeping youngsters amused.

He was a member of the Magic Circle, but to the delight of the children his tricks were very often in the Tommy Cooper mould, in other words they deliberately failed. He also loved trying out his magic tricks on anyone who was willing to let him. In this regard he followed the example of St John Bosco,[2] whom he greatly admired. When John Bosco, a peasant boy from Turin in the north of Italy was young, he learned how to perform magic tricks. He also learned to read. Nothing unusual about that, but in the early 19th century, when the rates of illiteracy were very high, it was something very unusual, especially for a boy from a poor family. He did this so that he could read stories to his companions, and so win them over to influence them for good. John Bosco also learned to walk the tightrope for the same purpose. He became very popular as a performer with his companions and friends.

I cannot improve on this selection of tributes from various tutors, and colleagues at Birmingham University,

> Sean was an outstanding young man. Even at eighteen he was already mature and integrated, a natural leader among the rest of the students. I cannot begin to say how much he meant to me, as a priest. For without realising it, Sean took much weight from my shoulders by the way he organised events, cared for people, and set a vivid Christian example by his almost daily Mass-going and his evident faith and morals. In all this he was fully alive, humorous, bouncy, witty and earthy. As regards the many female students he knew, he was a real gem; if only so many others could have learnt from him. I could go on in appreciation of Sean. Various people who lived with him have been ringing me, totally shocked. I am neither shocked nor surprised. I know that Sean would have been fully aware of all the risks and dangers, but would have known that his responsibilities to the people, and to the truth, must come before his own safety. I never knew him to be self-absorbed, even for a minute, and he was always blunt and forthright in matters of right and wrong. I am immensely proud of him, that he has paid with his life, working in Somalia for starving

---

[2] St John Bosco, also known as Don Bosco, was the founder of the Salesian Congregation.

and strife-torn people. I am personally happy that I spotted the talent he had, and gave him the opportunity to be the Catholic Society Chair.

Fr John Reid

I met Sean during the PE exchange with Charles University in Prague, in 1985, I think. It was a miserable week, that is to say, the weather was miserable, but the one memory I have of that particular exchange was Sean's drive and enthusiasm, and his sheer ability to ensure that everyone enjoyed themselves, despite everything. What an organiser, doer, creator! All these, and his passion for life, his exuberance, marked him out as an outstanding student, and clearly someone who would do great things in the future. What a dreadful, appalling waste. He was, in the very best sense of the term, someone who took goodness around with him and offered it liberally to all he came into contact with.

Tim Marshall

I interviewed Sean for his place at Birmingham. I note from my write-up following Sean's first term, that I viewed him as a natural leader, always enthusiastic in introducing new ideas for discussion, and clearly bringing out the best in the rest of the group. At Scarborough on his Geography field trip, once again I recall his willingness to join in absolutely everything, quickly emerging, again, as one of the leaders. Sean was one of the nicest undergraduates I have had the privilege to know in twenty five years. I was pleased that he was being so effective in putting his principles into humanitarian practice. His life was such a gift of life to others, and his death is such a waste.

Dr Peter Jarvis

Other colleagues wrote of his enthusiasm for life, his commitment; the sheer force of his ebullient personality, his warmth and generosity of spirit, enormously good-natured; the main problem is that one runs out of superlatives,

A most promising young man; of the highest ideals and principles; dedicated unselfishly to the well-being of others. A natural leader; perceptive, thoughtful, considerate and one who enriched the lives of all he touched.

Whilst we grieve at this tragic loss, we celebrate his short life, which was dedicated to the well-being of others and we know that he would want us all to strive to find forgiveness for those he sought only to help.

We cannot count the ways in which we grieve Sean's passing and our sole consolation is that he gave his life in the compassionate service of others and of his ideals.

Sean left Birmingham University in 1985 with a good honours degree in Sports Science and Geography, and the Monroe Sports Award. He then went to Exeter University in 1986, where he studied for his Post Graduate Certificate in Education. He also picked up along the way, coaching qualifications in basketball, tennis, swimming and soccer.

On graduation one might have expected him, on the basis of what he had said to Fr Brown earlier, to take up the opportunity to go to Africa. But he didn't. To the casual observer it would seem that all ambitions in that direction had disappeared, as he sought out a teaching post in England. More mature now, I expect that he wanted to gain some teaching experience before he set out for Africa. Sean had originally intended to teach at his old school in Farnborough, but since at that time he could not serve his probationary year at an independent school, he decided to try for a position in other Salesian schools. It so happened that Chertsey had a vacancy that suited him. He particularly wanted to teach in a Salesian school because he was very devoted to Don Bosco's system of education, with its basis in Reason, Religion and Loving Kindness. So he took up the position at the Salesian School, Chertsey, where he spent the next two years, teaching Physical Education, and became a tutor to Sixth Form students preparing for the Certificate of Pre-Vocational Education.

In reality he never abandoned his plan to go to Africa. He merely assigned it to the back burner. His friend and flatmate Paul Cowdery noticed this as he recalls,

During the time he was in his first teaching post at Salesian School, Chertsey, and although he enjoyed his work, you sensed that he was forming other ideas. It was those thoughts which ultimately led Sean to Liberia.

It was only after two years in the school at Chertsey that Sean felt himself ready for the challenge of Africa. Once again he approached Fr Brown. This time there was no hesitation on either side and soon Sean was on his way to Liberia.

Chapter 3

In Liberia with the Salesians

In those things which are for the benefit of young people in danger,
I push ahead even to the extent of recklessness.

Don Bosco

Sean arrived in Liberia on 13th February 1989. On arrival in Monrovia he was immediately assigned to St Francis School in Tappita, a secondary school of about 950 pupils with a wide ability and age range. Tappita is situated to the north of the country. He was introduced to the school community at the morning assembly on the 21st February 1989. His responsibilities were curriculum development, teacher training and the teaching of English, Religious Studies, Social Studies and Sport.

In these extracts from his early letters from Liberia we can see that Sean settled down very quickly, though at times there were pangs for the things of home. In 1989 he wrote,

> I really miss a good lump of cheese, not to mention a fresh glass of milk and a great crunchy apple. Things are very good, I think I'm going to be very happy. Arrived safely with all my baggage intact. I managed to get through customs with the help of a guide who negotiated a $10 fee with me. The Salesian place here in Monrovia is really quite something; they have a small Technical College, called Arthur Barclay, for students from 18 to 24 years of age. They have a lovely house on the site and a great cottage, it really is very well equipped: video, microwave in the house, shower and toilet in your own room. Tappita is certainly different, certainly more basic, but they do have showers and flush loos! I'll tell you all about Tappita once I get there. I've been jogging along the beach every morning, a good 40 minutes, which is really nice. Swimming, however, is really dangerous where we are, so we have to travel a bit to get a safe beach. I went to a football match yesterday. It was amazing, the football wasn't different, but watching the crowd was a real education. About a quarter of the crowd would be there to sell something; peanuts, plantain, chips, water, sweets, crayfish, kebabs, etc. One little salesman was about 3-4 years old. It's amazing how street-wise and independent they become so early on. I really feel conspicuously white. The people are exceptionally friendly and laid back.

This letter tells us so much about Sean. His optimism; he is not going to be *happy* in his new job but *very happy*. His enthusiasm; for what he observes of the school in Monrovia. His imagination; he is already describing Tappita from what he has been told about it! His observation; of the young children he saw at the football game. They were of special importance to him and he did not miss a thing of what they were doing. Helping these children and others like them was to be his mission, first in the school in Tappita, and then with the UN, in a wider context, for the rest of his life.

The friendliness of the people was to strike him more and more during his time in Liberia, as he grew ever closer to them and they to him. He was very much taken by this friendliness, the generosity of the people, their willingness to help in any way they could, and their stoic acceptance of their lot. He loved them for all these things,

> I'm only now beginning to realise the extent of the health problems here. It's true that the people are marvellously strong, with an incredible immune system. But I'm told that 70% of the population will have the malaria virus in them, with 20% at any given time, that's 150 kids in the school, actually suffering from the symptoms. Plenty of the children will have open sores and boils. The most striking thing is that they make such little fuss. There's no whining or moaning or attention-seeking. If you're ill here, you just lie down!

Sean was soon up to his eyes in work. He had his first break from school in mid-March when he went, with Br Donald MacDonald as his companion, to Monrovia, to collect a new pick-up truck for Tappita. Arriving back in Tappita, he immediately organised a talent show, where children were invited to perform anything of their choice. Sean himself kept the whole thing going with his patter and his bow-tie that lit up intermittently, to the great amusement of the children. He always had plenty of prizes to encourage participation. He had first perfected this technique while at school and university, when he travelled to Guernsey with his school's party for summer camp. There he amazed the holidaymakers on the expansive beaches, when he could keep a large crowd of school children enthralled for long periods with his quizzes and games. The holidaymakers initially looked with horror when a large horde of school children exploded onto the beach, but then stayed on to gaze in wonder and admiration at what they beheld. Some even returned to witness it again and to be entertained themselves.

Sean's fertile mind was always looking to the next event. Having hosted a talent show in March, he then planned to put on a Passion Play for the school and the village in April, on Good Friday. This was a major undertaking for anyone, with parts to be chosen, scripts to be written and costumes designed, but for someone who had only been in the school a couple of months it seemed impossible. Sean was nothing if not an optimist, and he set to work in preparing the very large cast. He took the part of Pontius Pilate himself, and had pillows strapped round him in the interests of authenticity. All went well until the pillows started to slip down. This lent a certain amount of humour to an otherwise very serious occasion. The play was performed in the open-air and by all accounts was an unqualified success. Sean would always succeed because he had no fear of failure. Failure is usually the result of fear of failure. People put undue pressure on themselves, because they think that if they do not succeed, others will consider them as failures. Sean never worried about these things.

Sean never had any difficulty in laughing at himself. The children were all that mattered, and as long as they enjoyed themselves and at the same time learned something from the theme, then he was satisfied and happy. His philosophy could have been based on the old adage, *the man who never made a mistake, never made anything.*

This was also a unique experience for the inhabitants of Tappita. They were now part of something never attempted before in their community, and unlikely to be again. During Easter Week, he introduced organised table tennis, football, basketball, and the high and long jump. These activities had taken place in the school before but never in such an organised way. The Resurrection, bursting into new life, was mirrored in the explosion of organised and new activities in the school and community. For Sean, sport was a major contributor to the general education and development of children.

Don Bosco declared that he was first, last and everywhere a priest. Sean could say that he was first, last and everywhere a teacher. As a schoolmate remarked,

> Even a casual knock-up in tennis became either a chance to win or to teach.

Table games such as snakes and ladders, chess and draughts soon followed. By April, after a mere two months in the school, he was organising a programme which allowed other schools and communities to take part in a wider network of games and sports. The American Salesians had donated a second-hand school bus to St Francis School, and Sean used this to transport his teams to play other schools. The teams all felt very proud arriving at rival schools in their very own bus.

The next innovation on his schedule was his weekly Press Report at assembly. It consisted of reports on regional and local news, sports and anything else that was of interest to the children and increased the knowledge of their surroundings, beyond their immediate neighbourhood. I think I can see his reasoning behind this. In one of his letters home he mentions a conversation he had with two 16-year-old boys, in which they had disclosed to him that they had never been outside the immediate area of their homes. In his own words he found this *mind-boggling*,

> I'm really beginning to get quite an insight as to how they live their lives. One boy Saturday Frazier, and his brother Wisdom, two 16 year olds both in my class, have NEVER been outside Tappita District. They have never walked past the immigration checkpoints on either side of town. It's mind-boggling.

The Press Report proved very popular with the students. Sean organised a competition for the best report, and a further motivation factor was instantly added.

Sean befriended a group of American Peace Corps Volunteers who were engaged in projects in villages throughout the region. They enjoyed each other's company, went for meals and a beer and discussed their projects together. Sean would sometimes go on weekend trips to see their projects for himself. You can be sure that while he enjoyed these outings, and they gave him the opportunity to be with people of his own age, he would also be looking at the projects to see what he could learn from them, and which could be introduced at St Francis School or in the other communities he was helping.

By May, Bingo had been added to his games to occupy the children. Again there were always plenty of prizes to be won. Sean organised a Sports Day on May 24th, the feast of Mary Help of Christians.[3] The day began with Mass at 8.30am, then a procession through the town, with bingo and football in the afternoon.

After this feast day, an addition to the school building was begun. Sean organised the youngsters in different groups, at different times, to get buckets and help fill the foundations. He knew the value of getting new

---

[3] The feast of Mary Help of Christians has always been celebrated in Salesian Schools.

classrooms as quickly as possible. They were necessary for teaching, and he was a man in a hurry.

Sean had been so successful in organising and training for games and athletics both in the school and locally, that he came to the attention of those involved with the national Olympic team. He was invited to prepare the team for the forthcoming Olympic Games. He was appointed national coach for the long jump and the javelin, training the athletes at the Samuel K Doe Stadium in Monrovia. However, he resigned from this position because he felt that the best athletes were not necessarily being chosen. It seemed to him that who you knew was more important than how good an athlete you were.

Everything in St Francis School was progressing very well for him. He was doing well in the classroom, exceedingly well in the organising of the sports and games, and inter-schools competitions, and was very popular with the students, who called him *Mr Sean*. His father had been to see him in May and they had spent some valuable time together.

Things became even better in July when he moved into his new home near the mission house in Tappita. Again he had no difficulty in getting children to help him move in, clear the ground for his vegetable patch, and a recreation area, and paint the house,

I've moved into the small cottage behind the church, it really is much better. I have an excellent shower and sink and the best view you could imagine out of my window. I've decorated the interior with Michelangelo classics. It really is a quaint little dwelling, kind of Latin American, with beige walls and rustic shutter windows. I've landscaped the ground around with the hope of producing a good lawn, from which I'll play croquet and golf, all of course in order to amuse the white man! I have prepared a wee nursery also. Here I'll plant some nice crispy vegetables like celery, carrots and parsnips. In fact, would you please send me out some seeds for those vegetables and some lettuce seeds too. THANKS.

I have also set up the Tappita Meteorological Station, or should I say I have stuck a rain gauge in the ground outside my house. I'm keeping a record of all the rain that falls during the year. We really have started the wet season now, and the roads are getting steadily worse. Mud pools have already sprung up on the road to

Ganta. They tell me that in the heart of the rainy season, August, Tappita can be cut off for about four weeks. All very exciting!

So, all in all I'm very happy and contented. The new cottage too is fine, kids will be popping in and out all day because they see it as Mr Sean's house now. They will sit and chat all day long if you let them. On Friday we're off in the big bus to Sanniquellie to play St Mary's Catholic School in all sports.

I've devised a totally unique wet weather suit. If you saw me in it, you really would laugh. Yesterday I was *jammed* as they say here, as it was raining and I had no cagoule or wet suit. So Mr Imagination here, took his British Airways suit cover and cut four slits in the arm and leg positions. With that trendy, designer, diagonal, full-length zip it really did look quite the part. The kids said I looked like a turtle.

Must go,
Love Sean.

PS When you have a chance to send a parcel, please would you put in,
those seeds
4 small metal trophies, see diagram, about 7 - 8 inches high
Table tennis balls, they are always handy
Couple bars of ZEST soap
Take the money out of my account. Thank you very much.

In another letter he writes,

Life for me is full and busy, and, needless to say, very enjoyable! I had a nice two-week break in Monrovia and am now back busy in the school. I've had the odd wee adventure too. On returning from Monrovia on my motor bike I got stranded in the middle of the bush, with no torch, no petrol, no water - it's a long story. I pushed my bike to the nearest village; by then it was 9pm. The people were so nice, they gave me bathing water, and pepper soap, and rice. They put me up in their deluxe model mud hut! I didn't get a wink of sleep due to various animal visitors in the night, i.e. rats, lizards and hogs; anyhow, the next day all worked out fine.

For the Independence Day celebrations, 26th July, Sean trained the dancers taking part. October 4th marked the feast of the school Patron, St Francis and was their Gala Day. The day opened with a procession through Tappita with dancing and singing, followed by internal games, and competitions against outside opposition. The day was brought to a close with another talent show. In November Sean organised a day of prayer for the 16-17 year olds.

He was further delighted by the news that his older sister, Theresa, was coming out to Liberia for a visit in November. Sean had prepared a meal for her arrival, to which the Peace Corps and the staff were all invited. It turned out to be quite something. Sean certainly knew how to celebrate special occasions, and knew how to help others to celebrate them too. He did not have to be fuelled with alcohol to do this. In fact, he was a very moderate drinker, did not smoke or indulge in any illegal substances. The joy of living, good company, making music and dancing, and similar activities were sufficient to make the evening pass joyfully, and often, hilariously.

It was near the end of the school term, and Sean was given another responsible task. He was asked to perform the closing ceremony at the school in the mission out-station at Graie, which he did with his usual panache.

With Christmas approaching, Sean decided on another production, a Nativity Play. Parts had to be written, organised, and the children auditioned. Costumes had to be acquired or made. With the prospect of the Christmas holidays coming up, the children once again entered fully into the spirit of the production. The play was to be staged in the open, and on the night the audience was treated to a great spectacle, culminating with the presence of a real new-born baby to represent the Child Jesus.

While all this was progressing in joy, however, dark storm clouds of conflict were gathering in the northern part of the country. In late December, there were rumours of attacks on homesteads and villages in the north, along the border with the Ivory Coast. The leader of the group of rebels, whose self-acclaimed mission was the overthrow of the corrupt President Samuel Doe,[4] was Mr Charles Taylor. His right-hand man was Prince Johnson, both of whom were to have a very severe

---

[4] Liberian head of state from 1980 to 1990.

impact on the country over the next few years. These men and their rag-tag rebel army had crossed the border from the Ivory Coast into Liberia. Their first conquest was the town of Khanplaye. From there they would move south over the coming months, covering the whole country and leaving a desert of destruction in their wake.

Meanwhile, Sean had left Tappita for his Christmas break in England. While he was at home with his family he was not idle. He gave talks and visited schools, to encourage the children to donate books, pencils, football kits, basketballs and anything else that they could spare, to help the children in Tappita. The result of this was that when he arrived back in Monrovia in January, he had a collection of these goods to take back north to Tappita.

But things had changed since he had left Tappita in December. Roadblocks were now set up. As he was making his way to Tappita, he was stopped at one of these roadblocks. The soldiers looked through his luggage and became very agitated when they discovered *spears*. They accused him of carrying arms for the rebels. Sean protested his innocence. A serious confrontation was only avoided when Sean gave the soldiers a demonstration of how to throw the *spears* which were, in fact, javelins. Sean was soon giving them a lesson on how to throw the javelin. The guards were delighted to join in.

Back in St Francis School the situation was now serious. There was a lack of food in the northern areas because of the unrest. A member of the UN, Mr Terry Lewis came from Monrovia to assess the food situation. It was decided to make St Francis School a centre for food distribution. Sean was needed to co-ordinate the food effort, and so his teaching at the school effectively finished, almost before the new term had begun. St Francis School was also now under threat, and in fact, was attacked around the middle of March. The children scattered to their homes or into the bush. Many of them were caught up and coerced into the war as child soldiers.

Paul Cowdery sums up Sean's idyllic days in Tappita,

> From my discussions with Sean during his breaks away from Liberia, I felt that this was the happiest time of his working life. Teaching in Tappita, seeking to give opportunities, and convert dreams into reality for those who might otherwise have had only

a limited view of what the world may offer, was something in which Sean delighted. This was his vision, which was soiled by the civil war that struck Liberia. Sean loved working with the children of Africa; he saw such great potential in all children, but working in an environment of limited opportunity and scarce resources, he was able to use his imagination and to see improvement quickly. I feel that it was his ability to see potential in all his students, and to devote his time and energy in developing that potential, which was the strongest link between the ideals to which Sean was committed and the Salesian ideals.

Chapter 4

In Liberia with the UN

The man dies in all who keep silent in the face of tyranny.

Wole Soyinka

On his return from his break in England in January of 1990, Sean knew that he could not return to Tappita and St Francis School. The school had been forced to close. He therefore offered himself as a volunteer to the United Nations, in Monrovia. This lasted from February to May 1990. Over the next eighteen months the three-month contract was to be his normal mode of employment. He kept it to three months because he wanted to be able to move back to Tappita when the St Francis School re-opened. He made that quite clear in letters to the Salesian Provincial at that time,

> For myself I have kept with this three-month renewable contract arrangement. It suits me as I retain the freedom to leave when St Francis School gets going again.

One young person who worked with him tells us,

> When the war started, he came down to Monrovia to do relief work. I remember very well, we used to take food to displaced centres, and other places. Sean was always down to earth with everybody, mainly children. He joked with them, always trying to make them happy, to make them know that indeed someone cared about them. Sean took us to the beach many times, held small parties for us, just to make us happy. Everywhere he went in Monrovia especially, on Broad Street, one could hear people calling his name: *Sean, Sean, Sean*. He organised matches and we played football at ELWA[5] sports ground. I can never forget Sean, never. Even when he was killed in Somalia it was a shocking thing for us in Monrovia.

Sean now began the nomadic life that would take him, over the next 18 months, to Senegal, Ivory Coast, Guinea, and back and forth to Liberia, before he went to Somalia in September 1992. He was first engaged in taking food and supplies to the north of the country, to Tappita and Nimba County. Mr Terry Lewis from the UN, as previously noted, with the consent of the Salesians, had established a distribution centre in St Francis School. Sean and his helpers moved frequently between Monrovia and Tappita on the food convoys. He also distributed food in Monrovia, and became even more well known in the city, where he was greeted enthusiastically whenever he appeared. Even though he was kept very busy during the day he still found time in the evening to visit Broad Street, where the young people hung out.

---

[5] ELWA is the name of a radio station (EL Liberia, WA West Africa).

One Liberian, who was in that group, described Sean as,

> Joking with the boys, giving them biscuits, trying to make them forget about the war. Sean has such a good footprint here that many people in Liberia will remember him for a long time to come.

Another Liberian, who was there at the time, writes,

> During this time, he was like a liaison between the mainstream UN office in Monrovia, and the Special Emergency Life Food distribution programme, known as SELF. This was the local agency for distribution of the UN World Food Programme. It was Sean who co-ordinated the work of SELF. In addition, he also mobilised us boys including some of his former students, to carry on the distribution of relief food in orphanages and other areas, where SELF's mandate did not reach. That's how orphanages and other needy groups began receiving food.

In Sean's world no one was to be excluded, even if the bureaucracy of large organisations had to be ignored or circumvented. I remember Sean once telling me, that in this situation, he felt that he had the best of both worlds. He was in touch with the Salesians all the time, and was therefore in touch with large groups of children, while at the same time he had UN trucks at his disposal. These trucks allowed him to gather the children together, and take them to sports and other activities that would take their minds off the war. He also had access to the main stadium in Monrovia. Later he was to write,

> One advantage of working in a rather high profile UN role is that one can get things done here without the usual hassle and procedure. We have seized nearly all our old fleet of UN vehicles, and last week I managed to get the leader of AFL,[6] General Boueno, to give us back our school pick-up truck. It is now safely in our compound.

To carry out this plan he needed helpers, and a great number of them. He quickly enlisted the help of those he knew and felt he could trust; the Salesians, his UN colleagues, particularly Michael Emery, an Australian, and some of his older students. With this workforce he would organise football matches, trips to the beach and other activities.

His first task as a UN worker was with UNDRO.[7] He began as a logistics officer, supervising the distribution of food along the Guinea-Liberian

---

[6] Armed Forces of Liberia.
[7] United Nations Disaster Relief Office.

border. The period he was to spend along the border areas with Guinea, Sierra Leone, the Ivory Coast and in Guinea itself, looking after the welfare of the refugees, was to be one of the most challenging, frustrating and traumatic of his life. He found himself challenged very severely on every level, physically, emotionally and spiritually, as we see from his letters at this time. He was to witness and be shocked by the cruelty of some people, and the corruption which blinded men to all considerations of pity and compassion. This would test all his reserves of patience, humanity, tolerance and forgiveness,

At present I am working in N'zerekore, Guinea, and also in the region of Macenta. I suppose there must be about 300,000 refugees here. The vast majority are from the Mandingo ethnic group. Some of the stories from the refugees are horrific, walking through the bush for days to reach the border. Many fled from Monrovia to Macenta via Sierra Leone. Rebels massacred many people in a Mandingo chiefdom in Lofa county. Vornjama witnessed the slaughter of Mandingos, perhaps 65 who stayed in the town, thinking the rebels would be friendly. Rebels have looted on a sweeping scale across the country. It is really tragic.

In the first few months of the conflict, the NPFL,[8] were respectful, smaller and tightly controlled, now it has grown out of control. Kids have weapons and tribal revenge is rife. It is so sad. In our house in N'zerekore we have six St Francis lads working for us, cooking, cleaning etc. They are Mandingo but very Liberian, and really want to get back to Tappita. All their best friends are from the Gio or Mano tribes. But quite frankly if they travel now, they will most probably get killed.

It has been good for me to see the other side of the conflict, to be associated with the people who really supported Doe. It gives me quite an insight into tribalism, and the divisiveness of African culture. It also depresses me greatly. Whole tribes can be misled simply out of the fear of their self-preservation being destroyed. When Doe died all the Mandingos ran through the streets of N'zerekore chanting, *We want Doe*. They refused to believe he died. Just imagine the contrasting jubilation in Nimba County!

With the death of President Doe the rebel groups lost credibility and motivation, the West African Peace Keeping Force ECOMOG[9] wanted to go home, and the country was left with thousands dead. One million people are now refugees, living out

---

[8] The National Patriotic Front of Liberia.
[9] Economic Community Monitoring Group.

of the country, and Monrovia, the capital, has been devastated, leaving about half a million sick and hungry.

It is important to understand, in the context of the above description, that Doe belonged to the Krahn tribe, while the Gio and Mano tribes were affiliated to Taylor and Johnson. In a letter to his family Sean wrote,

> Well, many things have changed since I last wrote. Things became impossible in Guinea Forestiere working as a Food Monitor. I was expelled from one country as I caught the chief of customs stealing refugee rice, and had decided to ask why.

Sean could be very impatient with those who did not share his high ideals. He explains that one of the volunteers, who did not want to rock the boat, and feared that the group would be labelled troublemakers, made too many compromises. Sean was immensely irritated by this, and did not feel that he was able to continue while his hands were tied. Unable to change this attitude and unable to do anything about it, he asked to terminate his standby contract so that he could move to some other area where he could do greater good. His superiors assured him that they had no problem with this, as they would utilise him in various other ways, before work started again in Liberia. However, the work he had done and the stand he had taken were to bear fruit,

> Our work was not in vain, all my field reports were sent to the head WFP[10] office in Rome, and Michael Heyn, the UN Regional Co-ordinator for West Africa, was totally supportive. After being ignored by the Red Cross, our own UN High Commission for Refugees and others, it was refreshing to get some support. Last week I received news that all the leading government figures in the refugee-affected zone had been re-located out of Guinea Forestiere, into positions of less significance.

This was a very considerable achievement in his fight against corruption, for the benefit of the refugees. Referring to work in Conakry on the Guinea coast,

> For the last week I have been down in Conakry working on emergency relief for the 10,000 refugees that arrived by ship from Monrovia. This last week has left such an impact on me. It's taught me so much about people, and human behaviour in times of desperation. The things I saw were almost unbelievable. Human beings have an enormous capacity for EVIL.

[10] World Food Programme.

Sean had never before experienced anything like this. He came from a background where the sanctity of life and family values were paramount. To experience the things that were happening here must have been very traumatic, and something he would have found difficult to come to terms with,

These 6,500 wretched war-torn souls had arrived in the port. They had travelled for nine days in the most appalling conditions. The Guinea authorities then made them wait on the dockside for up to four days without food and water, before being transferred to the central stadium where the relief agencies took over.

There were loads of police and army at the port, doing their security screening and immigration registration. I gained entrance to the restricted area, using my UN badge, where they were processing these arrivees. I saw soldiers and police on top of the container passing over a ten litre bottle of tap water, that had been freely got from a tap a few yards the other side of the barrier, and sell it to a refugee for ten American dollars. Soldiers would take a transistor radio from a refugee in return for some food. Their desperation was deliberately exploited to the full. I'm beginning to learn how to cope with situations like this. I hate it, I suppress my anger, I then do everything legally possible to change it.

Sean was never afraid to stand up and be counted, whether it was against bullying, cheating at games, corruption in services, or warlords. He just hated injustice,

The UN are hesitant to interfere with government responsibilities and, in my opinion, never go far enough on insisting on greater autonomy. But I found ways of beating the system. We are now ready for the next ship, which is due to arrive next week. Even if we can't speed up the government's slow registration, I now will be present in the off-loading area, with emergency food and water, eggs, bread, sardines, oranges. I've got the budget for it. The people may still have to stay in appalling conditions for a long time on the dockside, but at least they will get good free food and water, and the soldier boys won't earn one bloody cent!

Once these refugees arrive at the stadium they get food and medical attention and then, after a few days recuperation, are trucked to the various towns in the country. 90% of these refugees are of Guinean origin who were working in Liberia.

On Friday I saw the saddest thing ever; it has also given me powerful motivation to continue work in emergency relief. In the chaos in the stadium, one army truck arrived from the prison with seventeen Liberians, who had not come on the ship, but had been detained for three months in jail, after crossing the northern border into Guinea as fleeing refugees. The soldier said they were now fully free and should be put onto the trucks that were going back up to the border areas. I decided to look in the truck first. They looked like Auschwitz victims. They did not even have the strength to walk down off the truck. I knew they were at death's door and a three-day journey up country would kill them. I got a medical doctor to make a medical insistence that they stay at the stadium.

I then took responsibility for their welfare, and am still doing so. First we went to the medical centre where two were admitted straight away to a hospital. I went out and bought food for the rest, mineral water, bread and fish, oranges, bananas and nuts. They were so frightened they were not really sure how to handle this sudden transformation. They were walking skeletons, and their skin was covered with craw-craw, scabies I suppose. They smelt dreadful. In a private part of the stadium I got water for them to bathe in. We burnt their lice ridden clothes and got new ones. We got shavers to clean their heads, and provided slippers for their feet. After a while they began to talk. They had been arrested in July at the border and were accused of being rebels. None were from the rebel tribes, three were under sixteen years old and two over sixty.

(On the margin of the letter Sean had printed the words THEY ARE TOTALLY INNOCENT.)

Most fleeing refugees used to wear a red band on their arm just in case they came across a rebel attack, because this was a guarantee for protection. When refugees reached the border they discarded their red band. In these seventeen cases they either forgot or left them in their pockets. They were jailed and were never given a fair trial. They could not speak French and their own testimony was never translated from English. They were put in a room 20m by 15m with 85 other prisoners. They did not have space to lie flat on their back on the cement floor, so instead they had to lie on their side, which led to injuries. They were beaten and had to use one hole in the corner of the room to defecate. They received a bowl of boiled rice, no salt, no sauce, no nothing, every day. Their conditions violate all international standards. Their trial violates the Geneva Convention.

For myself, Guinea has been a really difficult experience. They have a very sophisticated, bureaucratic, highly secretive government and structure. In Liberia the relief agencies were fully independent and in control, here everything has to be ratified by the government. The corruption is just mind-blowing. I would say only 40% of the food is going to refugees. Some organisations collaborate with the government and in the end the refugees suffer. If you complain, you risk expulsion. Last month my Italian colleague from the League of Red Cross was expelled and I, as a UN monitor, was under house-arrest for one week. They were hesitant to expel a UN employee because of the repercussions. This was because we revealed that the refugee number in one town was only a quarter of what the government stated, and we carried out our own registration to confirm this.

On Saturday I caught the chief of Customs taking fifty sacks of rice from the Red Cross warehouse. Because I questioned the move, I was told by the government prefect that I had insulted the Guinean government and that they would draft a report against me. The UN here have been very weak, and, sadly, incompetent. So I have told my boss that I will not renew my contract after 23rd October, unless UNDRO[11] go back into Liberia before then. I may add that there is a strong possibility that I could be expelled before that date!

As indeed he was. He later wrote,

For the last four months, until November, I was working as a UN delegate with the refugees in Guinea. This country surpassed all others in its human rights violations. Sadly, the corruption masterminded by the Guinean government in the distribution of relief food was an evil to behold. Having been expelled by the government from the refugee zone for contradicting the Guinean authority's refugee figures, I found myself in Sierra Leone

---

[11] United Nations Disaster Relief Office.

planning the return of the United Nations back into Monrovia, a far more agreeable task.

After his experiences along the border countries with the refugees, and because he had been thrown out of Guinea, Sean was transferred back to Monrovia.

In December 1990, in a letter to Fr Michael Winstanley, Provincial of the Salesians of the GB province, he writes,

> I returned to Monrovia, in a US Navy helicopter with the first three-man UN team on November 15th. We have set up base in the British Embassy, and now have more than twenty workers, and a gradually increasing fleet of vehicles. The city is calm now, totally controlled by ECOMOG. It has taken them a long time to diplomatically or otherwise, push the AFL[12] and the ULIMO-J[13] back to their bases.

Sean then speaks of the refugee situation in the capital,

> In October there were 80,000 people here; now it has reached 400,000. You can imagine the growing pressure we are under to get food distributed. Since the cease-fire, people have been moving back into the city. Thankfully the gradual opening-up has also seen a movement of fresh food from the farms back into the city. But food prices are still extortionate. In contrast, non-edible goods are really very cheap. The looting has been extensive, but I suppose inevitable, when there are thousands of desperate people in a period of no real law and order.

He describes the scale of the devastation, but notes that slowly the people are beginning to go back and pick up the pieces,

> Michael Francis, the Archbishop, arrived the same day as myself and he has been busy running around the Catholic centres in the city, getting various people to clean up and temporarily secure the buildings.

---

[12] Armed Forces of Liberia.
[13] United Liberation Movement of Liberia-Johnson, as distinct from ULIMO-K United Liberation Movement of Liberia- Kromah.

In the next section of his letter we can see Sean's anguish at the plight of the children, and especially his pupils from St Francis School,

> Fr Larry Gilmore[14] told me that about 95% of our St Francis boys, and some girls, had joined up with the Taylor rebels, and that includes boys down to thirteen years old. I didn't want to believe it. But that's the reality. I suppose being male and Gio and living in Nimba, provides only one option for these kids. But still you can't help thinking, what happened to our attempts at Christian Education? What about our message of tolerance, forgiveness and love? I know now it means NOTHING when they find themselves at the centre of a deep-rooted tribal conflict. The old faith has taken a bit of a dive, perhaps in view of the madness that I have seen here, but I suppose that is all in the process of growth.

This obviously was something which caused him deep sorrow and great pain and anguish and tested his faith, but that faith was strong and deep enough to enable him to continue his work, even with renewed energy and commitment,

> I have had some difficult personal and emotional times, it is not easy seeing one of the small kids that you taught to play football, dressed in oversized army gear, shouldering a weapon of destruction, and then come up crying to you, because he now realises he's trapped in a ghastly, crazed environment.

One can almost feel his anguish. Everything he had worked so hard for; all the efforts he had invested in these youngsters, brought to nothing by the greed and power-seeking of evil men. It seemed more than he could bear,

> Because of having to do something to help one of my students, on 25th November I found myself in jail, under the orders of Prince Johnson. It nearly became a major political incident; with the UN ready to withdraw operations. Can you believe it? Thankfully the thing has blown over. The St Francis kid was released too, but not until after being thirteen days in Johnson's jail, with bruises to prove it!

Sean promised that he would do his best for his ex-pupil and asked Johnson to release him. Initially Johnson agreed, but then had his soldiers arrest them as they were leaving. They were brought back

---

[14] A Salesian priest from the USA who worked in Tappita.

Sean as Captain of Farnborough Salesian College with Anthony Byrne the Vice Captain

Sean - ever the Joker

Putting the melon!

'Mr Sean' trying to make them forget the war

Innocent victims of war

Sean negotiating for the distribution of food aid

The five religious sisters murdered in Liberia

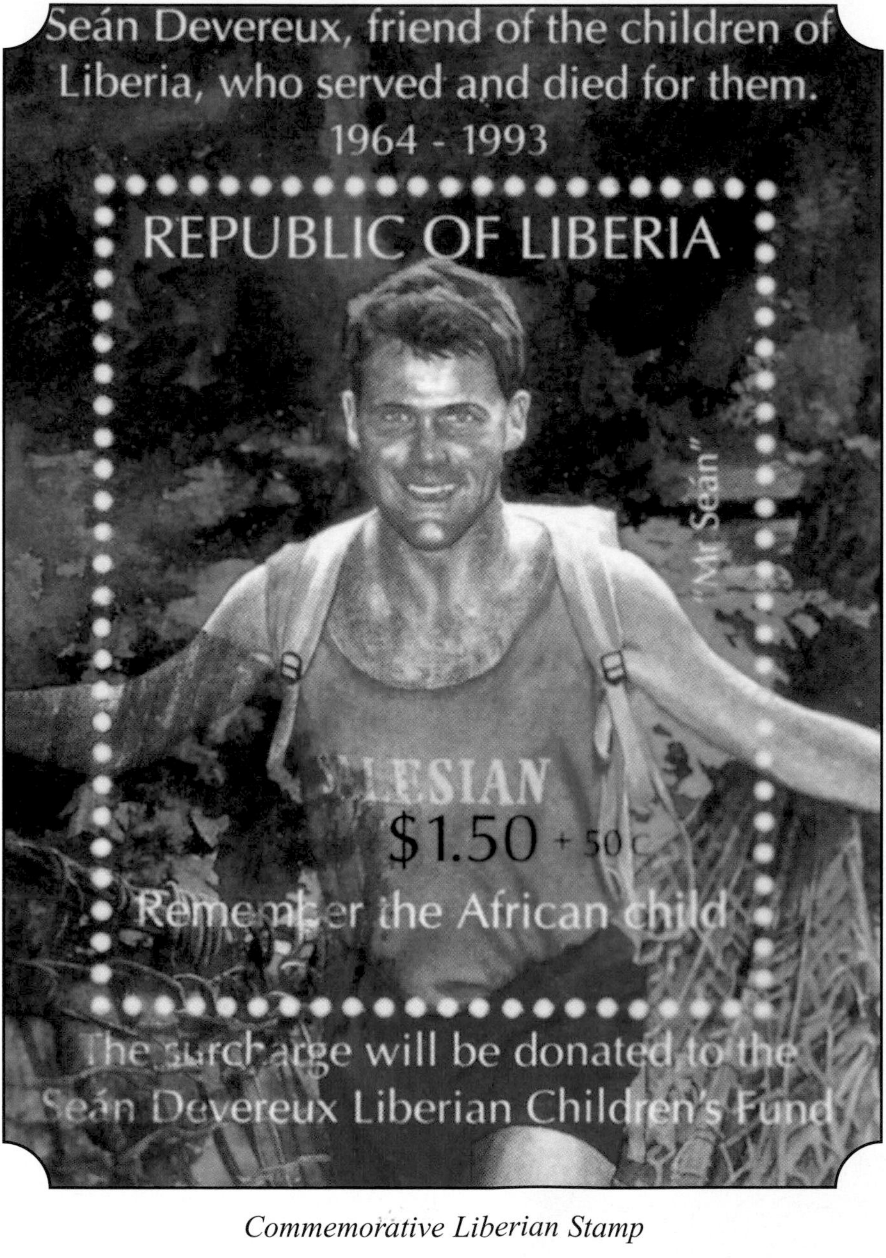

Commemorative Liberian Stamp

before Johnson, who had the boy beaten and Sean thrown into jail. Sean was released the next day, but it took two weeks of persistent endeavour before he could get the boy out.

Fr Joe Brown, who was with Sean in Liberia, recalls that he loved to tell how the jailer asked him why he had been put there. Sean replied that he didn't know. But the jailer insisted,

> I've got to put something down; otherwise they will shoot me.

So Sean said,

> Just put *Pending*.

He overheard another soldier ask the jailer what the newcomer was in jail for, to which the jailer replied,

> It's something very serious. He's been *pending*.

Only Sean could make light of such a potentially hazardous event. But it also shows how terrified these soldiers were of those in charge.

That Sean was aware of the danger he was in, can be gauged from the fact that he had the courage to go to Prince Yormie Johnson, the notorious rebel leader at his Headquarters at Gbarnga, to ask him for permission to take food into territory controlled by the warlord's soldiers. Others have said that Sean had gone to Gbarnga to a UN ceremony with Johnson, to mark a possible cease-fire. Johnson was a forbidding man; cruel, bad-tempered and unpredictable, often under the influence of drink or drugs, or both. He had a record that would frighten anyone. Described by someone as the *psychopath's psychopath*, it was he who ordered the butchering of the Liberian leader Sergeant Samuel Doe, himself no angel. He also ordered the making of the video of the process of dismemberment of Doe, which was then sold on the open market. It became a best-seller in Liberia.

Sean at this time was also organising games and athletic events for children from the various orphanages in rebel territory. His aim was to get these children away even for a few hours, when they could be reminded that they were children, who should be playing and enjoying themselves, not carrying guns and killing. Many of the children in these camps were being kept against their will and frequently plied with drugs, to give them courage for their acts of violence and killing.

When Sean arrived at the camp in Gbarnga, one of the boys, a fourteen-year-old conscript, a former pupil from the school in Tappita, pleaded with him,

> Please, please, Mr Sean, you have to get me out. This is an evil place.

He saw many more of his ex-pupils there too. He said that he found this frightening and sad. These boys whom he had seen playing football at school, were now carrying Kalashnikovs and Berrettas. They ran across to him, giving him a big hug, and asked to go back to school. When he heard from them that two of the boys from his class in Tappita were dead, he was devastated, more especially as they were, as he said, the gentlest type, not at all macho or aggressive. One used to go jogging with him every day, and was a good left winger at football,

> It is such a shame. This boy has been used in this conflict. Having been sad, I'm kind of angry now.

This was always Sean's greatest trial, to see his pupils engaged in the war. His friend, Michael Emery, said that he saw him weeping when he found out that some of his pupils had been killed in the war. He would say,

> To use children as warriors, that's really evil.

Even in these horrendous times, Sean's thoughts were still occupied with ideas for the children he so loved, and of how they might be protected from themselves, and the unhealthy wartime environment in which they were trapped. Many were now homeless orphans, and he could foresee the dangerous temptations they would inevitably be faced with. In his letter to the Salesian Provincial, he wrote,

> It may be wise to consider some new Salesian presence here. One possibility is working with the ever-increasing number of street kids. Now there are gangs of boys, homeless, that roam around Waterside, the Freeport etc. They are dangerously idle. We need to get an orphanage/boys town/sleeping/eating hostel, off the ground. I think more than ever this is a call for Don Bosco's work.
>
> Hope you all have a great Christmas.

His wish was to become a reality after his death, with the opening of the Don Bosco Homes project in Monrovia for the victims of the war and the rehabilitation of the boy soldiers.

He writes in March 1991,

> Life here has really lifted up with refreshing new arrivals of some relief workers. CONCERN[15] and GOAL[16] from Ireland are now operating; no doubt we will have a raucous St Patrick's Celebration. It's strange how St Patrick's Day is really celebrated when you're abroad.
>
> My actual work is very smooth running now. In our last distribution we managed to get rice, oil and beans out to 700,000 people, everyone got food. 163 distribution centres are now working, and our only problem is authenticating the registration. Some of the neighbourhoods are masters at creating ghost houses and inflating occupancies, so right now I whiz around the city with my 'criminal investigation squad', UN monitors, mostly ex-Tappita teachers. We have over 30 supplementary feeding centres in the city, and another 10 orphanages. UNICEF has just started a field hospital, which sees over 200 patients a day. So, all in all, the relief programme is working. My real concern now is the Liberians developing a dependency. Now we have to stop the general distribution and leave a Food-for-Work programme intact. If the country opens up we are faced with the prospect of thousands of returnees that could well start the whole problem over again, so contingencies are being made now. That's one reason why the UN are keen to keep me on. If I extend, it will be until May 31st. I am trying to get a break but it is really difficult.

Solutions were never stop-gap for Sean. While he was at pains to alleviate the immediate suffering of the refugees, it was their long-term well-being that was his priority. He wanted to prevent any possibility of a handout mentality. So he developed his *Food for Work* programme which he used here and in Somalia to such positive effect. It also helped the dependents get resettled in their homes. He already had the experience of rehabilitating 30,000 displaced Krahn people, who had fled into the high forests as a result of tribal killings. The programme, executed from Zwedru, which he had set up as a UN operational centre, involved general food and clothing distribution and farming assistance, through the distribution of seed-rice and farming tools.

---

[15] CONCERN is a charity working in many of the poorest countries in Africa and Asia in both long term development and emergency projects.
[16] GOAL is an international humanitarian organisation dedicated to the alleviation of suffering among the poorest of the poor in the developing world.

Sean, with his band of volunteers, continued his work of bringing back some normality into the lives of the people of Monrovia, by organising different events for the beleaguered inhabitants. Besides his normal work with the UN he could find the time, energy and enthusiasm, to persuade the UN to sponsor a Sports Fun Day for over 1,000 orphaned and war-traumatised children at the beginning of 1991. This venture of bringing together the children most scarred by the war, was so well supported by participants and helpers, and was so successful in bringing joy and happiness into their lives, that he was encouraged later in the year to organise a Monrovia Peace and Unity Fun Run. This seemed an outrageously optimistic venture, in the face of all the chaos, warring, killing and maiming. Nevertheless he was able to bring combatants from the war together for a Fun Run! Incredibly, about 10,000 took part, many more than he had anticipated in his wildest dreams. The whole thing was an unbelievable act of optimism, but he pulled it off. Later in the year, in December, he organised the first Monrovia Schools Sports Festival to be held in the country. All the while he was involved with the children around Monrovia. As his co-worker in Somalia, Caroline Tanner, later said,

> Sean was like a Pied Piper. He loved children and they loved him. He was a focus, a good organiser, a natural leader.

Another UN co-worker, Michael Emery concurred,

> Sean had a phenomenal gift with people, especially children. He loved children. I remember in Liberia, a four-year-old and a six-year-old walking for miles and crossing six checkpoints just to hang out with him, then trek home again at the end of the day. He had boundless energy and ideas. You can't imagine the effect of his magic bag of tricks. He was dynamic, he single-handedly organised the feeding of 750,000 people in Monrovia. By getting two teams to compete he managed to raise the amount of food moved from 150 to 800 tons a day.

This was a strategy that he was to use very successfully in Somalia also. Michael Emery continues,

> If he'd lived to be sixty he could have changed the world. He changed a lot of people's lives and did more than most of us could do in a lifetime. He had his heart in Liberia, and wanted to go back there when things had calmed down.

One of the tasks he was assigned by UNSCOL,[17] while in Liberia, was the organisation of the project for the democratising of the local food programme in Monrovia. This involved compiling and publishing a comprehensive election guideline booklet, as well as keeping the public well informed through the local media. A local team of 60 independent Election Supervisors had to be recruited, trained and monitored, to make sure that they were competent and above reproach. The security of the logistic arrangements for the day-to-day running of the elections had also to be guaranteed.

To make the process more understandable for the 60,000 principal householders, 67% overall turnout, Sean used a unique colour-coded multiple box system. In this way the 811 local elections were successfully managed. He wrote to his friend Ofieba about this operation in March 1992,

> Life is really fine, but I am at a crossroads. I've had one of the best stints, getting involved in the local elections, 811 of them for SELF,[18] throughout Monrovia. It was a hoot and just up my street. Now, sadly, UNSCOL won't extend my contract for another three months as requested, as they are only funding consultants for up-country work. Maybe this free two to three months is a blessing, I've been busy, in fact I've been running around like a fart in a fit for the last month, and this chance for reflection, holiday, rest, may do me good. I might even volunteer doing a bit of teaching work or youth work for a month or so, before going back to the UK.

One notices how aware Sean was of the necessity for reflection. He refers to this on numerous occasions. He was very aware how necessary these supports were in sustaining the spiritual life, and from which he drew the strength and the courage needed in his struggle against corruption and injustice. In this I feel that he drew immense inspiration from *The Prophet,* a book he obviously knew well and sometimes gave to his friends.

In 1991, Sean was delivering food, in his distribution programme, to Zwedru, which was the heartland of the Krahn people of which Sergeant Samuel Doe was a member. It was a *dead zone* after the death of Doe, since no one wanted to have anything to do with the clan, for fear of reprisals from the new leader, Charles McArthur Taylor. People had

---

[17] The United Nations Special Coordinator's Office in Liberia.
[18] Special Emergency Life Food distribution programme.

been killed and villages destroyed. Those who were left were hungry and frightened. Sean had to pass through a roadblock manned by Taylor's troops. He was stopped and the rebels started to take some of the food. Sean remonstrated with them. One of the guards jabbed him on the nose, taunting him and saying *you white man long nose*. Sean's temper flared and he bit the guard's finger. The gunman hit him. Sean retaliated, and knocked the soldier to the ground. The other guards piled in, hitting Sean with the butts of their rifles and tearing off his clothes. He was only saved when one of the young guards shouted,

Stop, stop! You can't do that, that's our teacher, Mr Sean.

This intervention probably saved his life.

One eye closed, badly beaten, bruised and bloodied, he nevertheless remained with his food convoy and refused to allow it to be taken by the guards. Eventually he was allowed through the roadblock. He remained with the food for three more days, to make sure that it went to the 14,000 starving people for which it was meant, and not to the gunmen.

But the event took its toll. He was weakened physically by the beating and was further threatened by Taylor, who announced on the radio that Sean was no longer welcome in Liberia. His life was now in danger. His superiors, fearing for his safety, decided that it would be better for him to first take a break in England, and then go elsewhere. It never occurred to Sean not to go back to Liberia, but his next destination was to be Somalia.

Before he left for home Sean had one more task that he felt he had to do. He had been appalled at what he termed *the killing fields*. This was an area of land, controlled by Taylor, at the junction of several roads, where victims had been taken by their captors, gunned down and left to decay. He wanted to give these people a proper, dignified burial. With the assistance of Michael Emery and some volunteers he collected the remains. Michael Emery said that collecting the corpses was a most difficult experience. When you can see the flesh and the clothes, then the reality of the person is brought home to you more immediately and vividly. The task was a gruesome one, only made possible because, as Sean said, the remains were those of someone's mother, father, brother or sister, and therefore, they deserved to be buried with dignity.

They buried these remains in three mass graves each with around 400 bodies. Sean had notices painted and erected over the graves, declaring that they were innocent victims of war. The notices were prepared and erected by ex-combatants from the Don Bosco Matadi Centre. At Sean's request, Fr Joe Brown performed the burial ceremony.

Sean knew that his parents were anxious and concerned about the state of things in Africa. They were wondering when he would find a career less dangerous and more remunerative. On such occasions, Sean was in the habit of saying to his parents, or anyone else who posed the same question, that though they might not understand what he was doing, he knew perfectly well where he was going.

His understanding of the part that parents should play in their child's life is graphically illustrated by the following story. On the day he left to return to Africa, he presented them with a little book entitled *The Prophet*, by Kahlil Gibran, a deeply mystical and philosophical book. Inside the front cover he wrote a message, asking them to read page thirteen. On that page they found the words,

> And a woman who held a babe against her bosom said,
> Speak to us of Children.
> And he said:
> Your children are not your children.
> They are the sons and daughters of Life's longing for itself.
> They come through you but not from you,
> And though they are with you yet they belong not to you.
>
> You may give them your love but not your thoughts,
> For they have their own thoughts.
> You may house their bodies but not their souls,
> For their souls dwell in the house of tomorrow, which you
> cannot visit, not even in your dreams.
> You may strive to be like them, but seek not to make
> them like you.
> For life goes not backward nor tarries with yesterday.
> You are the bows from which your children as living
> arrows are sent forth.
>
> The archer sees the mark upon the path of the infinite,
> and He bends you with His might that His arrows may go swift
> and far.

Let your bending in the archer's hand be for gladness;
For even as He loves the arrow that flies, so He loves also
the bow that is stable.

Inside that front page he had also added a further note to his parents, saying that they had achieved this admirably. It was a gesture of complete confidence and gratitude. Did he have a premonition of what was to come?

Chapter 5

The Liberians Speak

You have walked among us a spirit, and your shadow has been a
light upon our faces.

The Prophet

What impact did Sean have on the young people he worked for and worked with? The following are the reminiscences of some of them.

Sean, I remember Sean very well. He often took us to the beach after work. One day we asked Sean why he didn't like living in the expensive UN residential compound of River View, but rather liked to be in Monrovia. He said, *To live at River View is like being in Europe. I don't want to be in Europe. I want to be where I can be with you*.

He did not like people taking advantage over other people. He always stood for the truth. For example, whenever we went to distribute relief food to hungry people in 1991, Sean used to say to us: *This food is for the people and it must get to them.* He was a man of principle. Because he wanted to help people, Sean risked his life in helping them. He was a helper, a humanitarian. Whenever and wherever there was a need to help, he was there. Sean motivates me a lot, even today. He always advised us to be strong, to be people of principle. He always encouraged us and made us do our work. From what he taught us, I can stand up today and use my hands to work for myself.

I wept when I heard about Sean's death. I was in Ivory Coast when I heard on the radio that he was killed in Somalia. I did not believe it at first, because I knew the kind of person he was: a lovely person that wanted to help people and to be around people. He was a pace setter and he should have been alive to help more people. He gave himself for the cause of humanity. Although today he is dead, he is a hero. Yes, he is a hero and will be remembered by us all who worked with him in Liberia.

Matthew Gonkerwon

I first came across Sean when I was a mission boy at the Pastoral Centre in Gbarnga. Sean used to come down to Gbarnga from Tappita. Sometimes he spent the night there or passed through on his way to Monrovia. I later came across him in Monrovia in 1991 when I, and other young folk, worked on the UN relief food distribution trucks along with Sean. He was a very active fellow, always willing to work and was always there with the little ones, I mean the unfortunate children. His is still a household name for us, the truck boys, whenever we gather together in groups of two, three or more. Today there are structures or programmes in

Liberia named after him. We knew him to be a hard working person, lively, always laughing, joking with children. I remember once upon a time that Sean paid my school fees and also paid the fees of many other youths.

From the beginning when I first met him, he was involved in sporting activities in Gbarnga. When the war came, he came down to Monrovia and started doing relief work. We used to take food to displaced centres, and other places. We came together and held a Memorial Mass for him. When the work we were doing on the UN relief truck was over, I was then in 12th grade in St Patrick's High School, where I graduated in 1993. I went on to work at Don Bosco Homes. In all these places, I tried to imitate Sean, to the best of my ability, by being sincere and committed and hardworking. So I am happy that I came across Sean. I was such a beneficiary because Sean did help to pay my fees.

Cletus Noah

I first met Sean in 1990 when we were working on the UN relief truck team on food relief. In Tappita he was a teacher at St Francis, where he was heavily involved in sporting activities with the school team: football, basketball, volleyball. To be very frank, although Sean is dead, his memories are still fresh in my mind, mainly for some of the principles he stood for. One main principle I gathered from him was that he tried to treat everyone equally. For example, when orphanages began springing up, occasioned by the war, Sean took it like a responsibility to put life into those orphans, many of whom were abandoned, their parents could not be found anywhere around. He had a constant visiting schedule for each orphanage, and on Sundays we could take the orphans to the beach. He was a humanitarian without limit. I myself benefited from his work. He assisted in getting me a job with the CRS,[19] and this year makes me 14 years with CRS. Sean is the root of my employment.

His style definitely impacted on my life. Sean was one person who always wanted people to progress. When the UN relief work we were doing, was about to fade away, a colleague of his, thought it wise to forward the names of the truck boys for permanent employment. Sean said it was not a good idea, especially for those boys who were still in high school. He said our priority, as young people, should be education. Sean said it

---

[19] Catholic Relief Services.

was dangerous to go after cash because it would limit our education, and our future would be bleak. I admired him for that. Sean was a real workaholic, totally committed to whatever he had to do. He never compromised on anything that hindered his principles.

All of us owe gratitude first to Don Bosco for bringing him to Liberia, and to his family for allowing him to come. Without Sean's help some of us would not have achieved the things we have achieved today. Sean, for some of us, was the gap-filler. He left a positive mark. He helped us to do the right thing, and to make the right decisions.

John W Clark

My first encounter with Sean was in 1989, when our school, Carroll High from Yekepa in Nimba County, went to Tappita to play a series of matches against St Francis. I really got close to Sean because of sports. One of my friends told me that Sean was interested in sports. Sean had told this friend that nobody could defeat him in table tennis. Knowing that I was the champ then, in the inter-high-school table tennis tournament in Yekepa, I decided to challenge Sean for a match. So that was how I first came closer to him. At the end of the match I beat Sean in three straights.

Sean was a teacher, a sportsman, a humanitarian who worked for less fortunate children in society. When I worked with him, we were involved in the distribution of rice, sugar, salt, corn-meal, milk. Sean made sure that these food items reached the needy and on time. He did not like cheating. He liked people who were honest, and he saw to it that those who worked with him were honest people. He impressed me greatly. He clothed and fed those who were naked and hungry. Those of us who were young took clues from that, and today I am using that same method here at CRS. I have travelled to several countries working for CRS, and giving clothes and food to naked and hungry people. I have ventured into dangerous areas just to help the needy. These were things that Sean did and today there are still people in Liberia, who are carrying on the dream of Sean, helping the needy. So his coming to Liberia was not a waste of time.

Richard Davis

Chapter 6

In Somalia

Through the hands of such as these God speaks,
and from behind their eyes He smiles upon the earth.

The Prophet

In September 1992 Sean left for Somalia on what was to be his final assignment. He had spent a very pleasant break with his family, at their home in Yateley, and was now ready for the next stage of his life. Somalia at this time was one of the most lawless places on the African continent. It was governed by warlords, who with their personal militia, ruled by the gun. Sean, in his final letter to the members of his parish in Yateley, and the Salesians in England said,

> I have heard some refer to Somalia as the *Hell of Africa*, I suppose a fair comment but not entirely true. I took up a UNICEF[20] posting here in September after concluding my time with the Salesians and the UN in Liberia. It seems that I have gone from the frying pan into the fire, but I also like to think of it as an enriching, broadening experience.

Somalia was one of the African countries in the late 1980s and 1990s which was constantly depicted on our television screens, with its scenes of desolation, devastation, starving and dying people, particularly children. This catastrophe was attributed to drought and the consequent failure of crops. But Sean believed that this was not so. As in many cases of famine in the developing world, the cause of food shortages is not always a lack of food production, but a lack of distribution. It is a catastrophe caused, not by the infertility of the soil, or lack of rain or floods, but by man. Greed in over-cropping, over-grazing or de-forestation causes desertification, which in turn leads to water and wind erosion of the fertile surface soil, exposing the lower layer infertile soils. The result is disaster,

> No doubt you have been exposed to the horror pictures of starving children. Sadly, it is a reality that has been brought about by man's greed and not by natural disaster. There is no real drought in Somalia. It is a country, which prior to the war, exported rice and sugar in abundance; nomads wandered peacefully with their camels, goats and cattle, living a relatively healthy life.

Another great man-made obstacle to food distribution is war. Control of the food supplies can be a very potent bargaining chip in the hands of those engaged in war, as well as a lucrative source of income. Present day control of resources in some African countries is generally the prerogative of the strongest and most powerful, and is usually attained through the barrel of a gun.

---

[20] United Nations International Children's Emergency Fund..

The bigger the gun, the greater the power. The guns are usually wielded by warlords. As a general rule these warlords are affiliated to clans, or tribes, which then come into direct conflict with each other and provide the touch paper for fighting and civil war. Civil war is always the most difficult to end or even contain, as each tribe or clan seeks revenge on the other, in an escalating spiral of violence and death. It leaves a permanent mark on the population and the country. Sean gave details in another letter,

> The former dictator Siad Barre, and General Aideed, Morgan and Ali Mahadi are the usual names mentioned in this battle of power. Because of the greed and ego of these men, everything was turned upside down.

> The gun dictates everything here, and the biggest guns have the most power, Somalia now is simply lawless. The relief agencies, whose mandate is to reach the dying, no matter what, acknowledge that we are subject to blackmail and extortion. But perhaps in some ways by accepting this we are perpetuating the conflict. We are providing finance for these gunmen to go and buy more bullets which end up killing more people. The authorities, which vary from place to place, depending on which clan is in power, seek to involve themselves in our work, but only to squeeze us of every penny that we have. Essentially they are the black mafioso.

Obviously Sean found the situation, of the aid agencies paying warlords for security and transport, a great moral dilemma. It provided further cash for buying arms. It was probably one of the reasons why he felt so strongly that poor planning by the Americans in *Operation Restore Hope* had cost lives. He was not afraid to speak out,

> But one must add to the list: The US Congress, the former Soviet Politboro, and the Italian and British Parliaments. This noble collection of men and women, over the years, approved the production and delivery of weapons of destruction to Somalia. The greed starts here.

Sean saw these men, and the countries that supplied them with weapons, as the real enemies of Somalia and its people, as had been the case in Liberia. The warlords were simply common gangsters. They ruled the economic scene like the Mafia, *the black mafioso*, as Sean called them.

They controlled the guns, they controlled the food, they controlled the people by fear, with their technicals[21] and their ethnic cleansings of the different tribes. They controlled the food through their grip on the docks. The henchmen of these warlords took most of the food from the ports by direct or indirect stealing. In other words they stole directly from the warehouse, or employed the hired truckers, who creamed off a part of their load. It was then sold back to the populace at prices that were beyond the pockets of the ordinary peasants, who in consequence were left starving. The warlords in turn, waged war amongst themselves and against the government, leaving the desperate peasants homeless and destitute.

It was into this maelstrom of anarchy, starvation, unemployment and deprivation that Sean was pitched. As was his wont he lost no time in setting about solving the immediate problem, getting food to the starving, using the organisational skills he had developed in Liberia. The urgent priority was to get the food out of the port, away from the clutches of the warlords and to the areas where it was most needed. The rate of removal when he took over was about 150 tons a day. This was far too low, and besides it left much in the port area that could be looted. So he set about organising teams of workers and paid them in rice for their work. The more bags of rice they moved, the greater the amount of rice they were able to earn. Just as he had done with the games and sports at school, the teams were encouraged to compete with each other. Soon the amount of rice being moved rose to between 700 and 800 tons a day.

However, Sean was still troubled by the fact that the trucks they were compelled to use were very often owned by the warlords, a situation that he found galling. He knew, too, that they were open to corruption,

> UNICEF, like every other relief group, is forced to hire gunmen to protect their offices and houses. We hire looted cars that are escorted by armed men in order to move around. We pay through the nose, at every stage, to bring the donated relief items to the needy: at the port and airport for docking and landing fees, to porters to off-load the goods, to truckers to transfer the goods to the warehouses and distribution centres. But sadly, in many cases the beneficiaries are the market men and the various militia and not the innocent women, children and farmers who are the most in need.

---

[21] Mad Max style customised Land Rovers and picks-ups with huge guns mounted on the back. Driven by Technical Advisers who spent their time protecting journalists and charities, or killing them, depending on who had hired them.

Sean found the whole situation abhorrent. But faced with the problems on the ground, what could be done? Apart from bringing the situation to the widest possible audience, which is what he tried to do, he was outspoken in his condemnation of all concerned in this injustice.

Sean spoke out over the radio and in television interviews against the warlords, and the terror they spread with their killings, which he called a kind of ethnic cleansing,

> Perhaps we have got everything wrong then. Maybe we should all pull out until the Somalis with the guns allow us to work freely. What if they say no? Perhaps then the UN should send in 20,000 no-nonsense troops ignoring the warlords' objections, and impose a safety chain for the secure delivery of relief supplies.

> Perhaps we should ignore the warlords' arguments that we are imposing on their own sovereignty. They know, as well as us, that the country and its society has degenerated and fractionalised, to such a base level that arguments of sovereignty and self-dignity are now simply rubbish. I know from talking to the average Somali citizen that they are crying out for the UN to take over.

The warlords hated Sean. He spoke out about the way they targeted people from the local community with their *technicals*, and their *ethnic cleansing*. He spoke about the necessity for some UN force to establish a corridor of safety, which would allow the aid workers to travel, without harassment and without their paid bodyguards, from the port or the airport to their target famine areas. He let the local people know who their real enemy was. There is a very strong possibility the warlords feared that he might give the locals the confidence and courage to stand up to them. It could well be that the warlords were more worried about the local, rather than the international, community. What has international disapproval ever done in these instances? His friend Madelaine Winnett explained,

> He spoke to the press about eye-witness reports he had received of tribal killings, target killings, a kind of ethnic cleansing of more than 100 people by followers of Colonel Omar Jess on December 8th 1992, and his description of the massacre was widely reported. He was well aware of the dangers, but nothing could deter him from his work for the needy, especially the children.

The warlords also hated Sean because he organised the people. This was especially true in the port area of Kismayu, which had been overwhelmed by the chaotic influx of people from the countryside looking for food. He had put a structure in place. With the help of his colleagues and local leaders he set up a framework for distributing food to the needy, and provided health clinics and other benefits. He paid the workers in food and paid them according to the amount of work done. This incentive had given greater impetus to his work. It had allowed food to be distributed faster and with greater efficiency, to where it was supposed to go,

> UNICEF are involved in special intensive feeding and health care for the severely malnourished, and our supplies, brought in by the Hercules of the German and Canadian Air Forces are generally well secured. We tend to succeed in getting this relief through to the children. Thankfully the feeding centres are now full of healthy and noisy kids.

> The general food distribution by ship, however, is less successful. In our last consignment of 3,000 tons of wheat to Kismayo less than 30% reached the target groups. We paid $160,000 to trucking contractors, all armed militia of course, to transport the food, with elders from the various villages and towns, who were supposed to escort the items. The food in most cases did not arrive, either because the elders made a deal with the truckers to divert the food to the market, or because it was intercepted by a group of bandits with bigger guns. The one good thing is that the looted food does flood the market and the prices drop incredibly. Now one bag of wheat, 50kg, is worth 6,000 Somali shillings, about one US dollar, a price that many can afford, but still there are many with nothing.

As we can see from Sean's words, the warlords had been very influential in the port area. They took the food and sold it on the black market for large profits, or demanded protection money to allow a certain amount to get to its destination. The warlords were now being deprived of a very lucrative trade and steady income. They were little concerned about the hunger of their 750,000 countrymen, whose suffering Sean and his team were trying to alleviate. The organisation of the food chain, set up by Sean and his helpers, and the more efficient distribution of the food, meant that their source of income had now all but dried up. Like all thugs and bullies, they were not happy about it. Sean must have known that these two actions would put him in conflict with the warlords. Yet he chose to align himself with the vulnerable who were being killed, and the families, especially the mothers and children, who were being deprived of food. It was to cost him his life, and there seems little doubt that the order for his murder came from the warlords,

> Today in Somalia, in the Southern port of Kismayo, I cannot walk from my house to my office, a distance of 400 metres, without heavily armed bodyguards. Thousands upon thousands of men in Somalia have their own weapons, they tell me it's for survival. Boys of 14 years live out their Rambo fantasies, believing they are fighting for freedom. They are so blind, but who can blame children? I wander through the market, checking on the prices of looted UN food; wheat, rice, beans etc. and I see next to the bananas and camel meat, AK47's, Kalashnikovs, Berettas, M16's, Bazookas, varying in price from $75 up to $200, all made in the so called civilised world. Next door to my home is a shack with the sign SPARE PARTS. Sadly it is not for cars, but for weapons, again made in the civilised world. We have a lot to answer for, and you at home can do something by lobbying your MPs.

Sean was an implacable opponent of the arms-trade. To illustrate his point, he used to tell the tale of a gun fight between two families over a stolen camel, during which 35 people were killed. At the end of all the mayhem the source of the conflict, the camel, just walked off. As Sean pointed out, without guns you would have had a few black eyes and some bruises but that's all.

> The relief work here is extreme in all senses. The needs are massive, but the obstacles are also enormous. Normally the UN, ICRC[22] and other NGOs[23] have certain ground rules before they start to work, such as reasonable security on the ground; their own flagged vehicles that do not carry guns, and the freedom to move and work independently to bring assistance to people whom they decide are in need. Somalia is regrettably the exception.

> The reality is that the various relief groups stay and put up with the harassment and intimidation, because innocent children are dying of starvation NOW, and their presence does make a difference.

---

[22] International Committee of the Red Cross.
[23] Non-Governmental Organisations.

In Kismayo today we have 50,000 displaced people, mainly farming families, living in camps on the periphery of the town. They receive a cooked meal every day from ICRC, a dry ration would only be looted. Now we hope to provide transport back to their homes, with a resettlement package of food for two months, seeds for one year, materials to rebuild their homes, tools to farm their land, with trained Community Health workers to ensure the appropriate distribution of UNICEF drugs. By the next planting season, April 1993, we hope the displaced camps of Kismayo will have disappeared. But so much depends on security. These people will not move back to areas where there is fighting. The various clans must first agree to stop fighting. Time will tell. The aim is to resettle them back to their farms along a very fertile river valley, only 150km away, instead of reinforcing their dependence on us and allowing this pathetic waste of productive manpower.

As in Liberia, after a long and hard day's work, Sean could be found working with the children, playing with them, coaching them, encouraging them and entertaining them.

Life for myself here is very up and down. I get so frustrated and fed up when I have to deal with the authorities, the guards and the contractors. Their greed is sickening. In contrast, I get such a lift when I get a chance to move out into the field and see how the feeding centres and health posts are running, and to regain contact with the more gentle face of humanity. Last week we cleared the excrement and the mortars off the town's football field and had a soccer and athletics tournament for the kids of the displaced camps. The Somalis can really run, one clocked 12.5 seconds for 100m. Compared to the Liberians, they are useless at soccer. Salesian school Chertsey U12 team would have beaten their big lads with ease. Next to the football pitch is an open field with hundreds of small dirt mounds. These are the graves of children who died about six months ago. The contrast is so stark, but as I watched the energy and laughter of the children as they kicked the ball, it brought home to me the message that where there is life there is always hope.

The stadium in question had been used for many purposes during the war, and was not in a fit state to be played on. It had to be cleaned up first. I am assured, on very reliable authority, that Sean undertook the more nauseous aspect of this unpleasant task himself. Nothing was ever too difficult if it meant that there would be a place for the children to play, exercise and be themselves. Terry Lewis observes,

> Without doubt Sean had so many unique gifts, which endeared him to the thousands of people he assisted, and especially to the hundreds of boys that he helped and encouraged. He was someone they could look up to. He probably had done more for these young people than we realise. In countries where there are few good examples to follow, Sean was very special for them in the most positive way, their hero, their hope towards a better future.

He was so busy that he had very little time for rest himself. However, one occasion provided him with one such much-needed break from the grim daily grind that was his life, the wedding of his great Australian friend Mike Emery in October 1992, in Adelaide. He was Mike's Best Man. On his way back from Australia he found time to pen this letter to another of his colleagues in Liberia, Fr Harry O'Brien.

> October 7th 1992
>
> Dear Harry,
>
> Right now I am in Dubai of all places, in transit between Australia and Somalia, just having enjoyed Michael Emery's wedding in Adelaide. I only had about five days' leave from Somalia so I went for it and had the time of my life.
>
> Somalia is completely out of order; it resembles a society fighting back after a nuclear war. Apart from the obvious physical damage, the roaming bandits, with their personal greed, extortion and exploitation, are an evil to behold. The relief agencies are being taken for a ride here. The militia make ULIMO and the NPFL[24] look like angels! I know it's hard to believe.
>
> So basically it's a dreadful place to work, but I know the experience will be invaluable.
>
> I miss Liberia terribly, especially our wee house on Mamba Point with all the lads. I was lucky to get such a close relationship with Liberians in the last year, I learnt a lot. I will definitely come back in March 1993 when my contract finishes in Somalia.

---

[24] National Patriotic Front of Liberia (Charles Taylor's rebel group).

Harry, I hope all will be well with you this year and thank you for your support and friendship over the last four years.

All the best

Sean

The next time he was to have a break was over the Christmas period, 1992, when he joined up with his parents and sisters in Nairobi, Kenya. The whole family enjoyed a wonderful time together there, sightseeing, picnicking, white-water rafting. Once when they were reminiscing and looking over photographs, Sean showed the other members of the family a picture he had taken of the five Sisters of Charity who were later murdered in Liberia by the NPFL[25] forces. His parents were concerned. They reminded him that he was in a volatile area and would need to be very careful or he also could face the same fate. He remonstrated with them, and said that he knew what he was doing, and that he was well aware of the dangers. Nonetheless he felt that,

> While my heart beats I have to do what I think I can do, – and that is to help those who are less fortunate.

The family returned home and Sean returned to Kismayo on January 1st 1993. The following day he held a meeting with his staff in his office, and was returning in the evening to his house, when he was followed by a gunman and shot from behind twice to the body and once to the head. He died instantly. He was 28 years old. His assassin, though known, remains free.

Mark Sterling, speaking at the UN Memorial Service in Nairobi in 1993, declared that,

> Sean's passion for life not only motivated and influenced the work of colleagues and friends, but more importantly, his contribution directly affected the lives and well-being of many thousands of Somali women and children whom he came to serve.

> Sean was a man of action, who made his commitment to Somalia because he felt that his action could make a difference. From the time that he arrived in Somalia in September 1992, Sean's hard work, initiative and love for those he served, resulted in the saving of many Somali lives. He facilitated and supported health workers in vaccinating nearly 30,000 children against the killer disease,

---

[25] National Patriotic Front of Liberia.

measles. His support helped to provide essential life-saving medical services. His efforts in controlling the food supply maintained feeding services for thousands of malnourished children each day. He provided shelter and relief assistance to thousands of families displaced by war and drought, and helped countless numbers of other displaced families to resume normal rural life through the distribution of seeds, tools and other items, required to re-establish their households and restore their shattered lives. This was always his aim, to give the people back their independence and dignity and sense of worth, and so prevent a dependency culture arising.

Sean was the moving and guiding force in the development of a project, to support the resettlement of over 50,000 people who had been displaced, and were living in squalid conditions in refugee camps around Kismayo. Unfortunately, the project was not completed at the time of his death.

Despite the difficulties and insecurity of working in Somalia, Sean achieved much for the most vulnerable: the women and children. Sean's success in acting for children, in saving lives and giving them hope, directly reflect his exceptional human qualities.

His passion for life was infectious. Always an optimist, he was always looking for more, or new ways, to do more. No problem was ever too big, and no opportunity to serve others was missed. He was always there, the organiser, the mobiliser, the fixer. He was dynamic in both his working and personal life. Long working hours over, Sean would be arranging other activities: a football match or running races for children in the camps, teaching children a new game or a new word, or he would keep adults and children alike, tantalised with his jokes and magical tricks.

Sean had a sense of humour, a sparkle in his eye and a very easy way with people. He was loved and respected. With all these qualities it is not surprising that Sean assumed a leadership role among those with whom he worked. Within UNICEF he provided leadership to a growing team of Somali and international staff, ever encouraging them, motivating them, and forever devising ways to do more for children.

Sean was a also a leader among the international community of Kismayo. He was knowledgeable of the area and its peoples. He had respect for others and the patience to listen and learn. He was also highly principled and would not be compromised on what was right or good. He was always there to help others do more. He was well known, respected and loved by the Somalis of Kismayo, for his dedication and commitment to serving others. Sean's decision to serve those most in need, even if it meant great personal risk to himself, was a conscious act, reflecting his own sense of personal commitment. He had done so in Liberia, before coming to Somalia. In fact it was his success in Liberia, which qualified him to serve in Somalia, the most difficult situation of violence, anarchy and civil war in the world, at that time. Sean was an inspiration, not only as a relief administrator, but as a man with a compassionate heart and a keen mind. Above all he was effective.

Echoes of Ofeibea Quist-Arcton, a BBC correspondent in Africa, as she tearfully recalled in the film *Mr Sean*,

It is the worst thing that can happen to you when you find someone you love has died. Sean's smile, Sean's laughter, Sean dancing you off the floor, Sean talking to you seriously. I kept thinking that what he would really hate about having died was - he hadn't finished the work he had to do.

Chapter 7

A Rich Harvest

Shall the day of parting be the day of gathering?

The Prophet

Sean Devereux was the first British aid worker to be killed in the line of duty in Africa. His death caused world news, outrage and, consternation. The wall had been breached and the fear that others could now suffer the same fate was a real possibility, soon to be realised. Up to this point aid workers had always been regarded as *safe*, but this was no longer the case. A boundary had been crossed.

Sean's body was flown back to England for burial from St Swithun's Church in Yateley, where he had worshipped for many years. His body was first laid in the funeral parlour at Crowthorne, where family, relatives and friends had the opportunity to pay their last respects. It was here that I saw his body and the wound that ended his life. The following day January 8th 1993 at the Requiem Mass, the church was overflowing with more than a thousand worshippers. Fr Brian Jerstice, who had worked with Sean in Liberia, preached the homily. He reminded all present of Sean's life and work in Liberia. He based his final thought on the words of the opening hymn, *I, the Lord of sea and sky*,

> Here I am, Lord. Is it I, Lord?
> I have heard You calling in the night.
> I will go, Lord, if you lead me
> I will hold your people in my heart.

Fr Jerstice concluded,

> Certainly God called Sean, and Sean replied,
> Here I am, Lord.
> God called Sean far away, and Sean replied,
> I will go, Lord.
> God called Sean to serve his poorest and most abandoned children and Sean replied,
> I will hold your people in my heart.

Sean's father, Dermot, also gave a very moving tribute to his son, saying how they were not just father and son, but also very good friends, who used to go on cross country runs together. He mentioned how Sean kept telling him, *You're too old Dad, you'll never beat me*. Dermot concluded, *Sadly, in the race of life he has pipped me at the post again*.

The service was attended by many dignitaries from his work and the UN. After the service Sean's remains were interred in the Salesian plot in Ship Lane Cemetery, Farnborough, Hampshire.

Over the next couple of years Sean became a world-wide figure. Articles about his life in Liberia and Somalia appeared in papers and magazines. I collected over 150 such articles from daily and weekly papers and magazines from different countries. Memorial services were held for him in many places, including his old school in Farnborough, the school he had taught in, at Chertsey, Liberia, Somalia, the UN headquarters in New York and Dublin.

Within twelve months he featured in an Everyman production by Richard Alwyn for the BBC called *Mr Sean*. In November 1994 his life in Liberia and Somalia was portrayed in a Yorkshire TV docudrama entitled *The Dying of the Light*, part of the *The War Machine* series dealing with the arms-trade. Filmed on location in Ghana and Kenya, the producer, Peter Kosminsky, said that while he was filming the funeral scene, set in Nairobi, he noticed that almost all of the extras were in tears. On enquiring, he found that this was because almost all of them had been at Sean's memorial service, in Nairobi, 18 months previously. The location was only about 100 kilometres from Kismayo, and since there were 10,000 extras for the aid-giving scenes, Kosminsky declared that many of the Somalis had been there when Sean was killed. This incident is a remarkable tribute to the memory of someone who was so very obviously loved and appreciated by these people.

In Liberia his life was commemorated on a set of stamps along with the five martyred Sisters from the Order of Charity. He has had bridges, homes, schools and projects dedicated to his memory. His time in Africa and what he made of his life has been used in GCSE and A level religious syllabuses. A charity, *The Sean Devereux Liberian Children's Fund*, started by his sister Theresa, has raised many thousands of pounds for the construction of homes, schools and other educational facilities in Liberia, and elsewhere.

What was it about Sean that inspired such a reaction? I know he would have been very surprised by this. He would not have expected it. Why? Because he never wanted to be rich or famous. He would see this as a huge practical joke. Everything that he did was done in a natural way. Even things which would seem very peculiar if others did them, somehow seemed quite natural when Sean did them.

To all intents and purposes, and to the casual observer, he was just an ordinary guy. Although just an ordinary guy, he did things extraordinarily well. He had no airs or graces, no pretensions of being special. He was ever practical and down-to-earth. He accepted people for what they were and not who they were. He made friends easily and quickly, and he remained a loyal friend. He could laugh at himself, had a very good, and sometimes earthy, sense of humour. He loved playing practical jokes. He also had a competitive spirit, and could be impatient with those who wasted time, or were not on the same wave-length.

Wherever he went he was always the life and soul of the party, someone who spontaneously organised the fun. I noticed that when he entered a room he immediately attracted attention and you could almost feel his sense of happiness spreading. He possessed a very special charism. He was able to maintain this sense of fun without the help of any stimulants, other than his own enthusiasm. He was always upbeat and optimistic. Even when describing the horrors of the wars in Liberia and Somalia, he always counterbalanced the negative aspects of the conflict, with something positive, usually the laughter of the young people he was helping.

Sean's life has also brought into focus the power of good, of honesty, integrity, and the will to fight for what is right, and to do it cheerfully, determinedly and consistently as exemplified in this one man.

Sean gave back to many children their childhood. He also gave them back their confidence and self-respect. He employed many techniques in doing this. There are the well-documented soccer matches, athletics meetings and fun runs that he organised. There were also the less formal games, trips, and picnics on the beach, the after-work evening meetings and magic shows that he put on in Monrovia, where he hung out with the street children. These encounters provided a chance for Sean to teach them some new words, to give advice, to listen, and sometimes just to give biscuits. He kept the channels of communication open and the goodwill of the children intact, so that when the opportunity arose he was able to save them from degradation and death.

Sean had other ways of repairing the damaged confidence of the children. For some, who were too poor to buy shoes, or other items of clothing, and in consequence felt ashamed, he quietly bought these items. No one but the children and himself had to know. This simple act allowed the children to mix with their peers without any fear of being out of place.

Fr Jerstice relates an incident that he once observed. There was a war-traumatised boy, who wandered about in a zombie-like state not wanting to be involved or take part in anything. Sean befriended him, and through gentle coaxing found that he liked jumping. Armed with this information, Sean set about providing the circumstances that would allow the lad to take up the sport. The boy started and slowly found that he not only liked to jump, but that he was actually good at it. As he became progressively better, so did his confidence increase. He became cheerful and confident again. This may seem a very small matter, but in the context within which Sean was working, this was a major success. A boy's confidence and self-worth had been restored, and he was now able to take his place in society again. He was perhaps not fully recovered, but now travelling along the right road.

Not only did Sean give his time and energy to his charges but he also gave his money. After his death it became known that he had supported a good number of students at St Francis School in Liberia, by paying all or part of their fees. Sean believed in education, and he believed passionately that education is the only way for the poor to escape from their poverty. This had taken him to Africa in the first place.

Sean had other ways of winning the hearts of children. His clowning and magic tricks were always a guaranteed means of bringing the children together, and even the adults, to give them some happy memories and respite from the horror of the war. At Christmas he commandeered some UN lorries, transformed them into Father Christmas grottos, and cajoled and persuaded the other UN personnel to dress up in Father Christmas outfits. This was not easy in the sweltering heat. He persuaded them to drive around the town distributing presents, while all the children ran alongside chanting *Mr Sean*.

Mark Huband, author of a book on the Liberian civil war, said that he felt that Sean always knew that he was risking his life while trying to help desperate people,

> I was always amazed by his boundless energy and great imagination. He was always thinking about how best to put a bit of a spark back into the miserable, tragic lives of the people he was trying to help. They really appreciated it, particularly in Liberia, where his deep understanding of the people meant he really knew how to entertain, enliven and generally encourage

people, who deep down were facing enormous pain and suffering.

Two years after his death, Sean's father said,

I find some solace in the fact that Sean wouldn't live a lie: that he died because he wouldn't live a lie does help. It's easier to believe that his life had a meaning. I am sustained by seeing him through the eyes of others. I find myself thinking that when my life ends there will be no thoughts, no memories like that.

Another colleague of Sean, Hester Williams, writes,

In 1992, I served as a Social Worker and Tracer with the MSF.[26] I also came in contact with Sean at the J.F.K. Shelter. Very often Sean took the older children on the beach and spent time playing games with the younger children on the Shelter's campus. The children loved him. Sean Devereux was an inspiration to many young people in sports. I heard him many times on the radio encouraging and organising young people. He was a true humanitarian. Even though I was not a close friend of his, I admired him, he was not pretentious. He truly loved the African people. Kindly let his family know that his footprints are left in Liberia and when the right time comes, his marks will be revealed.

Paul Cowdery asks,

What was it that enabled Sean to develop such a powerful rapport with his pupils? I shared a house with Sean during his first year of teaching at Salesian School, Chertsey. Sean was dedicated in his lesson preparation, but it was his conviction that learning should be enjoyable which dominated his planning. Sean would not tolerate any disruption, but his approach was not that of a disciplinarian; he was simply convinced that what he had to give was valuable and that if his students co-operated they could learn in an enjoyable and creative environment. And what might Sean have been doing now? He was committed to action and not words. He had great qualities of leadership but I feel he would not have been content operating as a detached administrator within a large organisation. Sean had to be at the coalface, implementing his ideas and leading by example. These are just some of my thoughts of a friend whose presence has enriched so many people.

---

[26] Medecins sans Frontieres.

His school friend, Christopher Lloyd looks back with pride,

> Even now I still sometimes think of him and feel proud, not
> necessarily in the sense of proud to have known him, more that
> I feel proud of him because of who and what he was. He was
> simply the best of us. I think most of us felt this way. He wasn't
> too good to be true, he was just Sean, and that was damn good.

If God truly loves a cheerful giver then Sean must have been dearly
loved. In the service of the poor, the abandoned, the traumatised
children, he gave not only of himself, but of his energy, his compassion,
his time, his money. Michael Emery said that *if Sean had lived he could
have changed the world*. This was a sentiment I heard repeated by others
who knew him. Others said, that what would have disappointed him
most at his death, was that he hadn't finished his work. Of course, Sean
has changed the world, and did in one sense complete his work. His
death has brought his life into focus, reminding us of the evils of greed
for power and for money, leading to corruption, war, famine, suffering,
starvation and death. Sean's conviction about the evil of the arms-trade
reminds us of the words of Former U.S. President, Dwight D
Eisenhower, in a speech on April 16, 1953,

> Every gun that is made, every warship launched, every rocket
> fired signifies, in the final sense, a theft from those who hunger
> and are not fed, those who are cold and are not clothed. The
> world in arms is not spending money alone. It is spending the
> sweat of its laborers, the genius of its scientists, the hopes of its
> children. This is not a way of life at all, in any true sense. Under
> the cloud of threatening war, it is humanity hanging from a cross
> of iron.

Sean, more than anyone, saw the results of this arms-trade, and its far
reaching and long lasting effect on a whole country's well-being. He saw
a generation being lost either physically or mentally by the brutalising
effect of the arms-trade on the child soldiers. Sean witnessed this both
in Liberia and in Somalia. He spoke very forcefully against it. His words
have to carry some special weight; it was one of those foreign guns that
ended his life: a life dedicated to peace and serving others.